American Cars in Prewar England

American Cars in Prewar England

A Pictorial Survey

BRYAN GOODMAN

McFarland & Company, Inc., Publishers
Jefferson, North Carolina, and London

LIBRARY OF CONGRESS CATALOGUING-IN-PUBLICATION DATA

Goodman, Bryan, 1933–
American cars in prewar England : a pictorial survey / Bryan
Goodman.
p.   cm.
Includes index.

ISBN 0-7864-1540-1 (softcover : 70# glossy paper) ∞

1. Automobiles—Great Britain—History—Pictorial works.
2. Automobiles—United States—History—Pictorial works.
3. Automobile industry and trade—United States—History.   I. Title.
TL57.G66   2004   629.222'0941'022—dc22   2003019129

British Library cataloguing data are available

Cover images: *Front cover:* 1927 Buick Standard Six two-door sedan,
called the Dominion two-door saloon in England. *Back cover:*
The author with *(clockwise from upper right)* his 1900 Benz,
1926 Amilcar and 1913 Sunbeam.

Manufactured in the United States of America

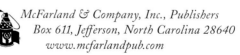

McFarland & Company, Inc., Publishers
Box 611, Jefferson, North Carolina 28640
www.mcfarlandpub.com

ACKNOWLEDGMENTS

Searching for and assembling these pictures has been made more pleasurable by the association it has brought about with like-minded friends, among whom are:

R. Bowers
Peter Brockes
Miss M. Burtenshaw
Elmbridge Museum
Farnham Museum
Christopher Finch
Kit Foster
Timothy Harding
Malcolm Jeal
Eric Parsons
Desmond Peacock
Nick Portway
Royal Commission on Historical Monmuments (England)
London Borough of Sutton Heritage Service

I wish that I could also thank those photographers of so many years ago who took these delightful pictures.

TABLE OF CONTENTS

Acknowledgments   v

Preface   1

Allard   7
Auburn   8
Bedford Buick   10
Briscoe   13
Buick   13
Cadillac   28
Case   39
Chalmers   40
Chevrolet   41
Chrysler   43
Cleveland Electric   48
Cord   50
Crown Magnetic   51
Dodge   52
Durant   55
Duryea   56
E.M.F.   58
Essex   59
Essex Terraplane   66
Flanders   68
Ford   69
Franklin   83

Garford   84
GMC   85
Graham-Paige   87
Grant   88
Harley-Davidson   89
Hudson   89
Hupmobile   92
Jewett   95
King   96
Krit   98
La Salle   99
Little   99
Locomobile   100
Maibohm   105
Maiflower   106
Marmon   106
Marquette   107
Maxwell   108
Metz   110
Mitchell   110
Moon   111
National   112

Noma   112

Oakland   113

Oldsmobile   118

Overland   125

Packard   130

Paige   136

Paige-Jewett   137

Peerless   139

Pierce-Arrow   140

Plymouth   141

Railton   142

R.C.H.   145

Regal   146

Reo   148

Ritz   155

Roamer   157

Rugby   158

Saxon   158

Stanley   159

Studebaker   162

Stutz   167

Terraplane   170

Vim   170

Walker   171

White   172

Wichita   180

Willys-Knight   180

Winton   181

Appendix A: Tax Discs   185

Appendix B: Registration Letter Codes   186

Index   193

PREFACE

When I came home from army National Service I bought my first car. It was a dreadful thing and quickly exchanged—on the advice of a good friend—for something older. That car was in Harrods' depository when bought in 1956, and my 1926 Amilcar has since been the most modern car in my collection. The next year, 1957, I discovered another one-owner car in a garden shed near my home town, and that 1900 Benz has since been the oldest car in my collection.

With marriage and children I needed something bigger and bought a 1913 Napier six-cylinder tourer. Later there followed a 1904 C.G.V., a 1911 Rolls-Royce Silver Ghost Barker landaulette, a 1908 Hutton Tourist Trophy racer (basically a four-cylinder Napier) and a 1913 Sunbeam sports tourer. Only the Sunbeam and my first two cars remain with me today.

In addition to collecting old cars I have pursued the somewhat less expensive hobby of collecting early motoring photographs. Sharing those photographs with friends has given me much pleasure, and with this book I hope to share that pleasure more widely.

Like most English enthusiasts, my knowledge of British and European motor history is greater than my American car experience. Fortunately in my efforts to describe American cars I have been aided by American historian Kit Foster, who checked my work and offered corrections and suggestions. Kit is a friend gained through the Society of Automotive Historians (a worldwide group based at 1102 Long Cove Road, Gales Ferry, CT 06335-1812 USA), and I am indebted to him for his paternal concern that I get things right. As research consultant he has had to overcome the problem that the Atlantic Ocean lies between us, and yet I could not have had a better consultant. I record my sincerest thanks to him.

The motor car evolved—and is still evolving; it did not appear fully formed and reliable in 1896, but developed slowly over time. Yet it is a very modern phenomenon. My grandfather was born only ten years before Carl Benz made his first drive.

1

Germany, with Benz and then Daimler, was the birthplace of the motor car, but the place of its infancy was surely France, which was strong in the last decade of the nineteenth century when the British were forced to be weak. England had a law requiring that a vehicle propelled by anything other than horses must be under the control of three men, two on the vehicle and one walking ahead to handle any horses encountered. At first this was not as silly as it might seem. The man at the back controlled the boiler (hence the word "chauffeur") and the going and stopping of the vehicle. The man at the front could only steer and pray! Almost the only vehicles on the roads were traction engines, which sometimes towed a road-train consisting of a grain threshing machine, the drivers' living van and a water cart. One can imagine that such a sight would terrify Mrs. Doe's pony, so the man on foot was very necessary too. The result was the suffocation of any development of the private car. If one was limited to the speed and range of a man on foot, it was not worthwhile to develop a car capable of overtaking a pedestrian!

This law, the Locomotives on Highways Act, was repealed in November 1896. In celebration of this emancipation, the pioneer automobilists of 1896 decided to demonstrate that the car was already practical. They organised a run from London to Brighton, a distance of fifty-eight miles to be covered in a single day! One third of the participating cars were French, but two Duryeas were also entered, one of them driven by J. Frank Duryea.

Even before this first London-to-Brighton Run a few Britons had bought cars in Paris and driven them on British roads, teasing the police. Charles Rolls (later to be famous with Henry Royce and a pioneer aviator) was a rich young undergraduate at Cambridge owning a Peugeot. It is reported that he set out to do the first Brighton Run but broke down and failed to be at the start. His would have been the only Peugeot on the run.

Soon England had its own makes: Lanchester, Daimler, M.M.C., Napier, and others. The imports continued, however, and as the United States truly got rolling, American cars were well in evidence in England, as this book demonstrates.

The needs and uses for cars in America and England were not the same. In England, towns are close, and although the roads between were not good they were certainly usable. American towns were farther apart, and the roads between them were unpaved and sometimes impassable. For use outside towns American cars needed to have a track to match the horse-cart ruts. This was not important in Britain.

By 1914 the ratio of cars per head in America (one to 80) was twice that in the United Kingdom. In the period 1908–1919 more than 40,000 cars came to England from America while only 881 went the other way. Let us not forget, however, that for nearly half that period England had a war on its doorstep.

After the Great War, there was a great hunger for cars in Britain. Many servicemen had learned to drive during the war and had their demobilization grants to spend. Factories, however, were not immediately able to get back into car production. England owed debts to America, which had not been attacked in the war and had introduced moving production lines to further lower prices. In 1915 the British chancellor of the exchequer, Mr. McKenna, had imposed a tax of 33⅓ percent on complete cars imported. Nevertheless, two out of every five cars on British roads in 1919 were Fords assembled in the factory at Trafford Park, Manchester, where the company had established itself in 1911. To circumvent McKenna, Overland sent cars over in pieces to be assembled with Crossley in Stockport, Manchester. Chrysler had an assembly plant at Kew, west of London. General Motors and Durant started factories in Canada so that their cars would be "Empire-built," which reduced the McKenna duty by one-third. In 1925 General Motors bought itself a British manufacturer, taking over Vauxhall. Hudson was also a prolific assembler here.

The first American cars had right-hand drive, but is it odd that nearly all the world's cars were right-hand drive? No. A coachman occupied the right side of a carriage box to allow room for the whip to be swung outside the carriage, and it was because he needed to see beyond his team of horses to pass carriages in the opposite direction that keeping to the left was preferred.

In America, few horse-drawn wagons were driven from the box. Controlling a team of oxen or horses on foot one would walk on the left, so preferring to pass to the right. Similarly, if riding postillion one rode the left-hand horse. Having read about early American roads one is tempted to suggest that riding a horse might have been more comfortable than sitting on the box of a coach. Britain's most famous carriage, the Coronation Coach, is driven by postillions, but until 1901 this carriage was in the hands of a coachman on a box. Readers might not be surprised to learn that we British have never had any problem about which side of the road to use—but I am not setting out here to discuss the origins of the rule of the road across the world.

A dissertation on car registration (what an American would call a license plate) demonstrates the British motor historian's advantage. Registration numbers are assigned to a vehicle and stay with that vehicle for its life. The plate is not changed when an owner sells the car or moves, even if he moves from England to Wales, Scotland or Northern Ireland. The number plate in an old photograph often offers useful information—though there are exceptions, of course. From the very beginning, in 1904, owners could have their numbers transferred to later cars. A friend in my home town has FX-3 on his current car. This number was on his grandfather's 20 h.p. Rolls-Royce in 1905, his brother has FX-4. Dennis cars (they were later better known for fire engines) were made in Guildford in Surrey but were often registered DB, which were the letters for the County Borough of Stockport in Cheshire. My own Amilcar was sold new in Rome in 1926 and must have carried Italian registration. In 1929 its English owner brought it back to London, where it was given the 1929 London number UU-997, which it carries to this day though I do not live in London.

With coachbuilders we are not so lucky. One does not see coachbuilders' plates on the outside of British-made bodies. Only by opening the door and reading the sill-plate can one confirm the maker's name. This is not the case in the United States or on the continent of Europe, where plates were usually fitted outside. (Surely the modern fad for wearing clothes with the maker's label stuck on the outside cannot have any connection?) Most of us interested in the pictures in this book would like to think we recognize the works of some constructors or at least know the country of origin. One could suggest that only in America were tourers marketed with permanent tops. Only in 1930s Germany did tops fold so poorly that they were then still higher than the top of the windscreen and only Vanden Plas achieved, without fail, a top that folded to the horizontal. One could continue in this field of bombastic comment.

Something else which makes the compiling of this book more challenging is the history of the camera. At the start of the century there were plate cameras producing pictures of superb quality. With the twenties came smaller, more portable cameras, producing lesser-quality photos of cars which themselves had become less special.

In this book are represented many makes, but surely not all of the makes that arrived in England. Most pictures are from my collection, but among the many who have helped me with this book I particularly thank my friends Tim Harding, Michael Worthington-Williams, Peter Brockes, Kit Foster and the late Eric Parsons, who have given me generous access to their collections. There are inevitably photographers of many years ago that I cannot thank but would have liked to.

Research and identification of old photographs is made easier in the United Kingdom by our system of registrations. These commenced on 1 January 1904. Counties (and some towns and cities) were assigned one or two letters each, to be followed by up to four figures (e.g., AB 1234). When this format had all been used (from 1932) a third letter was added in front of the other two and the numerals limited to three (e.g., AAB 123). In 1953 this combination finished and the system reversed (123 AAB), putting the numerals ahead of the letters. This lasted only ten years before being reversed again with a suffix date letter added (AAB 123 A). In 1983 this was reversed again (A123AAB), and as I write this in early 2002 we have a completely new system.

The letter codes for the original one and two letter districts are listed in the appendix.

I do hope readers will enjoy this glimpse of life in England with American cars before the Second World War.

Bryan K. Goodman
Fall 2003

ALLARD

Above: Twelve Allard cars were built pre–World War II by Sydney Allard, owner of Adlards Motors of Putney, a Ford dealership west of London. These were specials based on American Ford chassis and using Ford V-8 or Lincoln V-12 engines and split-axle front suspensions designed by Leslie Ballamy.

This Allard is being driven by Sydney Allard on May 15, 1939, at Prescott Hill Climb, Gloucestershire, where he won the "over 3,000 cc" class with a time of 53.21 seconds.

AUBURN

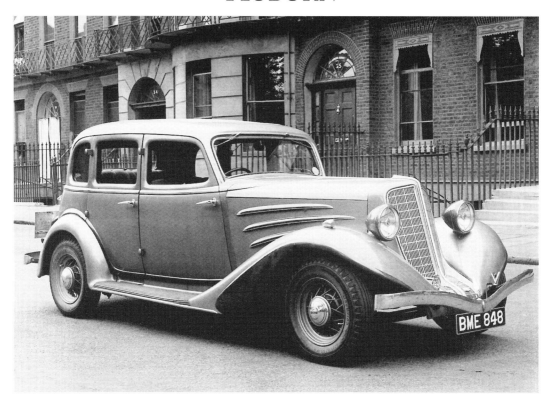

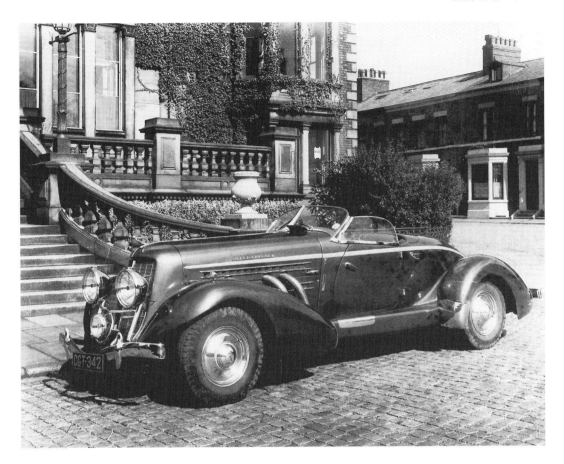

Above: A similar car to the speedster at opposite bottom. But look what one Englishman could do to it! The front-fender-mounted sidelights were a requirement and the semaphore direction indicators (just rear of the hood) necessary for this size and class of car, but the Lucas P100 headlights would not have amused the designer. Later in this book a 1939 Ford has suffered the same treatment.

Opposite, top: A 1934 Auburn sedan with two-color front fenders, surely a most unusual feature.

Opposite, bottom: Only a year later, in 1935, Auburn introduced the supercharged eight-cyclinder dual ratio speedster. In 1934 Gordon Buehrig and August Duesenberg were asked to design a new Eight with new styling but economically. Some body panels were carried forward from the 1934 car. The stunning 851 and 852 models comprised only some 600 cars and the make did not survive into 1937.

    The British Agents R.S.M. (Automobiles) were in London's Berkeley Square which is probably the location for this promotional picture.

BEDFORD BUICK

Opposite, top and bottom: David Buick was born at Arbroath in Scotland, but was taken to Detroit when he was only two. In 1908 Buick was one of the original members of W. C. Durant's General Motors. Buicks were sold in England from 1907, but starting in 1909 Flint-made chassis were shipped to England to be bodied by British Bedford for the British market. Here are some examples, though the first two 1909 Bedford Buicks look to have American bodies. The police sergeant is about to see the chauffeur into the very cold mother-in-law seat.

Bedford Motors of London's Westminster announced this "modified American design built in England" in November 1909. The company is not to be confused with the name used by Vauxhall in Bedfordshire from 1931 for its commercial vehicles.

Above, top and bottom: Two very British bodies on 1911 Bedford Buicks; equipment includes a Stepney spare wheel on the two-seater.

Top, left: Pre-First World War wheels that were not detachable were the cause of many road-side delays as tires were removed, punctured tubes mended, tires replaced and tubes re-inflated to 60 pounds or more. It was a dirty job too.

British towns have always been much closer together than American towns. Instead of miles of mud, British roads were of stones patched with more stones which, under heavy wagon traffic on iron wheels, broke into sharp flints. The mixture of flints, broken horseshoes and horseshoe nails was not a good surface to drive over with primitive pneumatic tires!

The Stepney rim carried a pre-fitted and inflated tire and this would clamp to the outside of any road wheel so the journey could be completed with the punctured tire hanging in place to be repaired after journey's end.

Opposite, top and bottom: From 1914, a landaulette and a two-seater Bedford Buick. The belt line with cane finish is a typically English feature accentuating the horizontal line which took over in 1911–1914 and persists today.

BRISCOE

Above: Another lesser make that lasted only five years and yet managed also to export to England. This family appears very happy with its 1920 Briscoe Touring Model B4 with a four-cylinder 24 h.p. engine. There had been lady drivers since motoring began, but there were more after self-starters became general in the twenties.

BUICK

Right: A 24 h.p. and an 18 h.p. Buick car climbing Box Hill in Surrey. The road is little changed today.

Above: Three Buick cars taking part in the Motor Club run from London to Brighton. In the front is an 18 h.p. Buick with Mr. Frank Eason driving, and Mr. and Mrs. Horace Goldin sitting at the back. Mr. John L. Poole is at the wheel of the second 18 h.p. Buick, with Mr. de Reeder next to him and Miss Annie Purcell behind the driver. The last car is the four-cylinder 24 h.p. Buick.

Left: 18 h.p. Buick. *Right:* 24 h.p. Buick.

Opposite, top: 18 h.p. Buick Chassis.

Opposite, bottom: A Buick D-4 truck chassis of 1915 or 16 converted to dual rear wheels for use in the war effort. A four-cylinder 141 cubic inch engine was used.

The location of the spare wheel rim must have made access for the "1 attendant" most awkward. When war came in 1914 very many larger cars were requisitioned by the government. Bodies could easily be removed for truck, ambulance or even armored car bodies to be substituted. Some owners of coachbuilt bodies kept them when the chassis were requisitioned in the hope that they could be refitted to those chassis after the war.

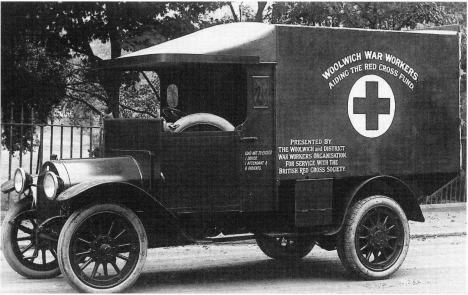

Above: The window shape is typical of the coachbuilder Regent Carriage Co. of Fulham in south-west London. This one is on a 1920 Buick. A large tool-box is provided below the foot-step.

Opposite, top: The date is 1918 and this Buick is photographed in Waterloo Place in London's West End. Wheel discs are fitted. The lamp covers are presumably for advertising and not up-market black-out covers unless the photograph pre-dates the end of the war.

Opposite, bottom: Still in Waterloo Place, London, a Buick Series D of ca. 1921 with drop-head coupé body by T. H. Gill of Paddington, London, supplied to Mr. R. Delpech of the Triplex Safety Glass Company. Note that the British coachbuilder is happy to leave the cantilever rear springs exposed whereas the American offering would have a convex valance to conceal them.

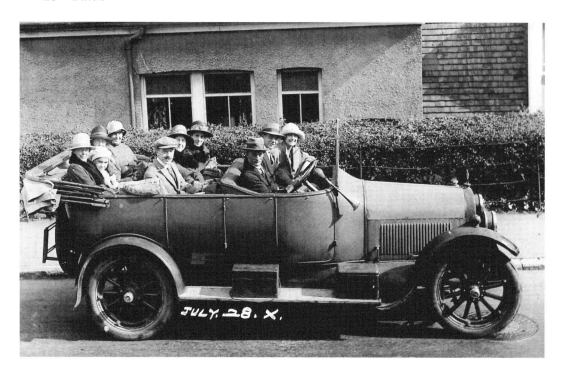

Above: The hiring of cars and charabancs for holiday outings was very popular in the twenties. Charabanc is a word of French origin and means a vehicle with several rows of seats. Where every row had its own access without doors it could also be called a toast-rack bus. (In England toast slices are placed on edge in a rack to keep them crisp.) Here a Buick with cantilever rear springs has been fitted with three rows of seating. Before departure a commercial photographer appeared as if by magic and on the party's return picture postcards of the outing were for sale, hence the photographer's reference written on the negative. Similar photographs appear elsewhere in this book.

Left: A big Buick, perhaps the six-cylinder model of 1923, carrying an all-weather body by William Osborne & Co. in London.

DE LUXE 3 SLEEPER, PRICE £125.

Top and bottom: Happy holidays in 1928 when one could pull off the road on a seaside headland and set up camp. The car is a 1924 Buick 24-45 five-passenger touring and the camping trailer is by Eccles of Birmingham (from where the Buick is registered) with its mock leaded-light windows and plywood body. Below is the interior of a similar trailer. Caravanning, as the English call it, became popular in the twenties, giving great freedom at manageable cost. It is still popular today.

 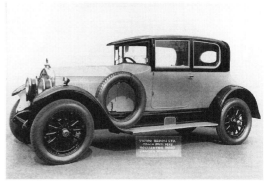

Left and right: The coachbuilder Victor Broom of Camden Town, London, was active only in the twenties but built on some prestigious chassis. The two-door design is surely the more attractive of these two Buick Model 24s. The four-door body is also pictured in this book on a Hupmobile chassis.

Above: What a very English and very twenties scene. A picnic in the bracken with freshly brewed tea from a china teapot. The men wear jackets and ties and the lady has a hat. The photographer has hung his or her camera case on the radiator cap which is surmounted by a Boyce Motometer water temperature gauge. That the car is a 1924 four-cylinder Buick is almost incidental to the scene but the V-windshield and roof luggage rack show British character.

Top and bottom: This Buick Standard Six Touring export model was driven from New York City around the world in the period from December 20, 1924, to June 23, 1925, a journey of 16,499 miles. Each Buick dealer drove it across his area and it is seen here outside the showrooms of the London distributors.

Below is another Standard Six Buick in Bell Street in Reigate, Surrey, outside the shop where today the owner's grandson Christopher Finch still sells bicycles from the same premises.

Above: This is a 1927 Buick Standard Six two-door sedan which was called the Dominion two-door saloon in England. It was "finished in beautiful light blue Belco—price £425." The picture is taken in the hamlet of Allerford, between Exmoor and the Bristol Channel in North Devon.

Opposite, top: The showroom of Wood's Garage at Holstein Hall in Weybridge, Surrey, displays seven Buicks. *Opposite, bottom:* A Buick Series 121 chassis hidden under a four-seat convertible Weymann-patent fabric body by Harrington of Hove in Sussex. The diver's-helmet front fenders were in vogue; the modesty-louvers along the base were a French influence, and on this style of body also served to connect the front fender/hood paint color with the rear fenders. The whole car is not a thing of beauty.

Above: Strange that some of these British-bodied Buicks are without the bumpers that were standard at home. This six-cylinder car has provision for only one wind-shield wiper and its sidelights have slipped even lower than on the home product. It still does not look comfortable to see an English body—this one by E. D. Abbott of Farnham in Surrey—on an American chassis, or should this English-man say an American chassis under an English body!

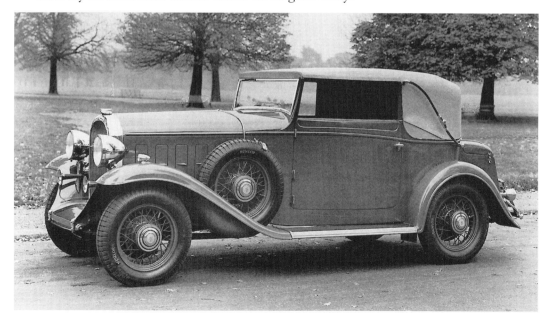

Opposite, bottom: This 1932 Buick Standard eight-cylinder chassis with convertible coupé body by Carlton Carriage Company in London is still without bumpers.

Below: Various European touring club and roadside recovery badges adorn the front of a 1934 Buick. Top right, one can see the semaphore direction indicator fitting which had become necessary to comply with British traffic regulations.

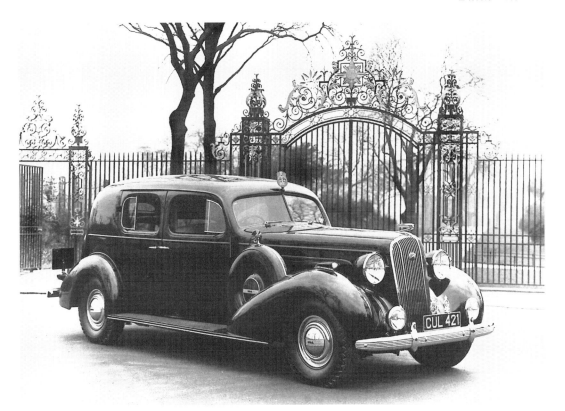

Above: King Edward VIII came to the British throne in January, 1936, as a very popular King, aged 43. But he had been courting an American divorcée, Mrs. Wallis Simpson, and abdicated his throne at the end of the year to marry this now-twice-divorced lady. The throne passed to Edward's brother George VI, father of England's present Queen and husband of the Queen Mother, who died in early 2002 aged 101.

The car is a 1936 Buick model 90L limousine with a custom body whose most noticeable feature was the omission of the rear quarter-light windows. The car came from the McLaughlin-Buick factory in Oshawa, Ontario.

It must have proved some embarrassment to the British distributor Lendrum & Hartman that arriving at their showrooms on the same day and from the same boat was another Buick Model 90-L limousine destined for Mrs. Simpson as a present from the husband she was so shortly to leave for the owner of the customised version of the same car.

Opposite, top: A Series 90 Buick limousine of 1934 with dual sidemounts and rear luggage rack.

Opposite, bottom: The Duke of Kent (1902–1942) was the fourth son of King George V. Like his older brother Edward VIII he favoured Buick cars and here is his 1936 245 Limited limousine with English headlights and hub-caps. Beside the Buick is his 1936 4¼ litre Bentley saloon by Hooper. The body was a saloon with a divider.

Above: This 1939 Buick Century Model 61 four-door sedan, sold in England as the Roadmaster, is seen probably in London.

CADILLAC

Opposite, top: A car from Cadillac's first year, 1903, and already in England. It used a horizontal single cylinder engine by Leland and Faulconer. Note the absence of any registration number. These were required from January 1, 1904.

Opposite, bottom: A street scene in Sittingbourne in Kent where a 1903 Cadillac is outside a bicycle shop. Above the shop are advertisements for Singer (cycles and cars), Michelin tires and Pratt's gasoline.

Above: Mr. W. S. Gilbert, author of *The "Bab" Ballads* and half of the famous Gilbert and Sullivan light opera partnership, bought first a Locomobile, then a 12 h.p. Napier, then a 16 h.p. Napier. He then acquired the 9 h.p. Cadillac seen at left with 1904 Middlesex registration. Mr. Gilbert is shown in his 20/32 h.p. Darracq landaulette (right) with body by Holland and Holland of London, bought in the summer of 1906. Mrs. Gilbert is in the Cadillac of which Mr. Gilbert spoke very highly, also testifying to the utility of the Stepney wheel which was actually in use on the far rear wheel at the time of the photograph.

The house is Grim's Dyke in Harrow Weald, Middlesex, built ca. 1886 as a half-timbered Elizabethan-style building. The dyke itself had already existed for at least 2,000 years.

Left: A Model M Cadillac with side entrance. The Honorable E. W. B. Portman and his wife had an identical pair of 8/10 h.p. Cadillacs at their home, Hestercombe, near Taunton in Somerset. Mrs. Portman's car has a water- and wind-proof apron fitted over the cowl and surrounding the steering column. Mrs. Portman's Cadillac is today back in Florida.

Above: The Fairmile Inn is at Escott on the edge of Exmoor in Somerset. The 1906 Cadillac is Somerset registered. On the left the horse droppings and water pump would lead one to believe that the stabling was still for the more normal form of transport. The Cadillac's horizontal single-cylinder engine was still located under the seats, the hood and dummy radiator serving only to give the appearance of an up-to-date car.

Right: Sir Charles and Lady Barrington and family, with their Cadillac cars.

Top and above: These are Cadillac Model M Victoria tourings of 1907. The second car carries a Surrey (PA) registration ten years younger than the car so the picture is post–World War I and the number may have been transferred from the owner's previous car. The body is surely of British manufacture.

Above, top, middle and bottom: The Automobile Club of Great Britain and Ireland (ACGBI and in 1907 to become the Royal Automobile Club) introduced the Dewar Trophy, presented by Sir Thomas Dewar in 1904, to be an annual award for the most outstanding technical achievement in automobiles.

In 1908 the RAC monitored the stripping down of these three identical Cadillacs, each into 721 separate components. These were then jumbled and the cars re-assembled and driven around the Brooklands track. For this proof of the interchangeability of parts Cadillac was awarded the Dewar Trophy for 1908.

In 1912 new Cadillacs with Delco electric starters fitted as standard were tested by the RAC for 1,000 starts, winning the company the Dewar Trophy for the second time.

Above: A merry group of seven set out from the French Horn public house during the war in a 1913 Cadillac Four.

Opposite, top: A boy in an Eton collar sits behind the driver also in a stiff collar. From the early years of the twentieth century owners had been adorning their cars with mascots, which included teddy bears, toy black cats and policeman dolls. This 1912 Cadillac Four has Scottish Ayrshire registration but most interesting is the aeroplane-engine-and-propeller mascot surmounted by a toy teddy bear. Until 1911 Rolls-Royce had no mascot, and it was to counter these poor-taste adornments that the company introduced the "Spirit of Ecstasy" that year, though for many years it remained an optional accessory.

Opposite, bottom: The *Autocar* magazine for July 26, 1913, described this as a "special two-seater made for Mr. Harden-Jones of Liverpool by (coachbuilders) J. Blake & Co. of Liverpool." The Cadillac picture was also used in an advertising brochure for Warland Detachable Wheel Rims.

Top: A British army sergeant with a 1915 Cadillac V-8 with a military camp in the background. *Bottom:* This car looks so British and pre-war and yet it is a 1918/19 Cadillac Type 57 with 90° V-8 engine. Detachable wheel rims were obsolete in Britain by 1919. The bell-shaped brass headlamps are electric but of pre-war style. So are the front left-hand tire and the steel-studded right-hand tire, designed to be non-slip on muddy roads but very skittish on pavement. The photographer was in Sidcup in Kent, but the coachbuilder is unknown.

Opposite, top: The interior of the Cadillac showroom at 24-27 Orchard Street, which lies between the south end of Baker Street and Oxford Street, London W1.

There is a battery in the box on the floor so perhaps the engine could be turned for demonstration, but with no exhaust system present it could not have been started. Charles Kettering had perfected the electric self-starter on the Cadillac of 1912 but even just after the war such starters were still a novelty in London. Charles Kettering was a director of Cadillac for the rest of his life.

Right: This Englishman assumes that Americans do not have a tradition of taking their private cars overseas, but for the British this has been normal holiday practice since the 1890s, with so many European destinations so close. Only since the 1960s, shortly before the arrival of drive-on ferries

to Europe, was the customs papers process done away with. There was an AA (Automobile Association) and an RAC (Royal Automobile Club) representative at every port (and at many continental ports too) to help members handle the car paperwork. Here a 1928 Cadillac with prominently mounted AA badge is presumably having its engine and chassis numbers checked before embarkation.

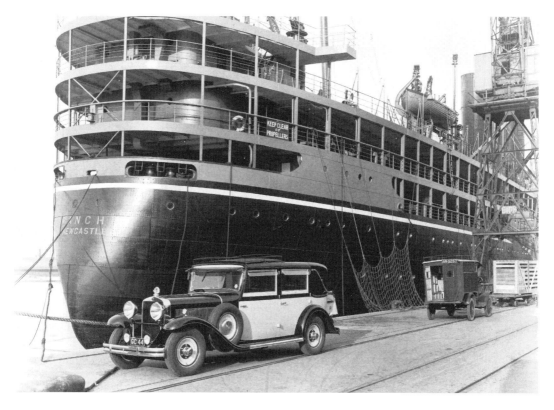

Above: The chassis is by Cadillac; it was made in late 1929 so it is a 1930 Series 353 V-8. The limousine body was built by Lancefield Coachworks in West London. The rear top-irons are for decoration only but the roof-rack has been put well forward to preserve the landaulette illusion. It has a sun-visor and semaphore direction indicators and the separate rear luggage trunk is designed to be detachable and taken into one's hotel room. It is finished in the body-color of the car.

Both the Cadillac and the Ford van are London-registered so this might be London Docks.

The Cadillac's mascot *(close-up at left)* is a cast glass "Longchamps" model horse's head created by René Lalique in Paris. Though not so mounted on this Cadillac the mascot was normally mounted on a base containing a light bulb to illuminate it at night.

Above: A 1932 7·4 litre V16 Cadillac.

CASE

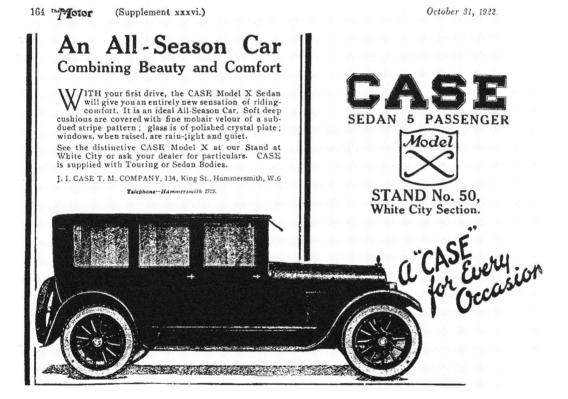

Above: An advertisement from *The Motor* in October 1922. J. I. Case is better known in the United States for agricultural and construction equipment. Cars were made from 1911 to 1927.

CHALMERS

Same Engine—Different Body

This is the Chalmers two seater — as great an achievement in car construction as the one that made the name famous. A gay little runabout that shies at a repair shop because it so seldom needs one.

The "Hot Spot"
Chalmers
America's Favourite Six

embodies the Hot Spot and Ram's Horn idea that makes even the worst petrol give every ounce of its power. It is practically vibrationless and as smooth and silky on the road as the better known four seater, and is fitted with the Bosch magneto.

Price £750   AT GREAT
                    PORTLAND ST.
EARLY DELIVERY ASSURED.

Trial runs arranged in rotation.   Fix one to-day.

Maxwell Motors, Ltd., 116, Great Portland St., London, W.1

Above and left: The Chalmers-Detroit became simply Chalmers in 1910. This is a Model 35-C of 1919/1920 with 45 h.p. six-cylinder engine. The body is English as is the haystack in the field behind.

Opposite, top: A smart English coupé body on a 1914 Chevrolet chassis. This is the Series H four-cylinder. It has similar belt-line treatment to the 1914 Bedford Buick already shown.

Opposite, bottom: Unregistered and carrying an enormous football is this ca. 1918 Chevrolet. The location is St. Helier on the Channel Island of Jersey. Despite a letter to the local paper no explanation for this unusual scene has been found.

CHEVROLET

Above: This Chevrolet four-cylinder with 1922 Surrey registration is seen outside a newly half-timbered pub in the Surrey village of Shere. This car was made seven years after W. C. Durant used his Chevrolet company to take control of General Motors.

Opposite, bottom and below: Chevrolet was a very popular make in 1920s England. These examples are from 1923 and 1925. General Motors took control of Vauxhall in England at the end of 1925 and of Opel in Germany in 1929.

CHRYSLER

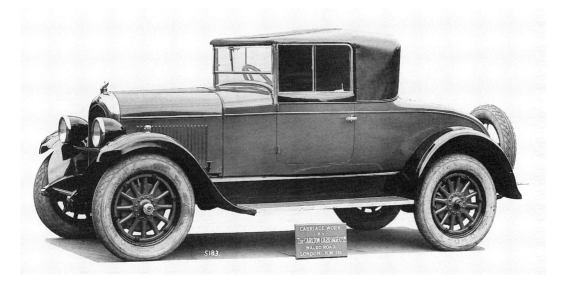

Above: The English doctor's coupé body sits oddly behind American headlamps and over the American wheels and fenders of this 1926 Chrysler Model G-70 Six.

Above: A 1928 registered Chrysler roadster. It has English Lucas lights: sidelights with the Lucas logo in the center and P100 headlamps with the triple-bar bulb mounting incorporating a bull's-eye lens. The car also has knock-on hub caps for center-lock wire wheels.

Above: The Brooklands Aero Club badge is at the center on this 1928 Chrysler's badge bar.

Above, left and right: The Chrysler Series 70 convertible coupé was built only in rumble-seat form with these distinctive louvers. The wire wheels and rear luggage rack were extra. The builder of the body is unknown.

Top: A 1931 Chrysler convertible coupé Series CD Eight fitted with English head-lamps. The car is parked in St. James's Street, London. Pall Mall starts beyond the taxi and the Ritz Hotel is near the top of the street behind the photographer. St. James's Palace is in the background. *Bottom:* Only 1,000 of these 1932 Chrysler CI six-cylinder convertible coupés were made, in rumble-seat form only.

Opposite, top: The family that bought the Chrysler Series 70 convertible (on page 45) in 1930 replaced it in October 1933 with this Chrysler Six "Kingston" sedan.

Above: The De Soto SE four-door sedan was sold in England as the Chrysler Croydon. The white disc carries Chrysler advertising but is not legible from the photograph.

George Burtenshaw & Son of Reigate in Surrey were local coachbuilders but in the 1930s turned to general car sales, particularly Austin and Rover. This photograph was lent to the author by the sister of the young Miss Burtenshaw seen here. Apparently her feminine charms assisted car sales at a time when women were not often seen in motor car showrooms. George Burtenshaw was a keen old-car man in the thirties so the car in front of the De Soto is probably his De Dion Bouton.

Above: Known in England as the Chrysler Kew Six in 1938, the car has a Plymouth body and mechanicals shipped from Chrysler in Canada. The Dodge Six of 1938 in this book is similar.

CLEVELAND ELECTRIC

Above: Stormount Castle in Belfast, Northern Ireland, the home of Mrs. C. E. Allan, pictured opposite in her Cleveland Electric.

Opposite, bottom: Mrs. C. E. Allan in her Cleveland Electric car photographed in 1900 in front of her home, Stormount Castle, Belfast, in Northern Ireland. Mrs. Allan was an artist; her husband was a director of a Belfast shipbuilding company and drove a 16 h.p. Milnes-Daimler car. The cars were built by Cleveland for Elmer Sperry and were known as Sperrys from 1900 to 1901. The steering tiller also controlled acceleration and braking which was soon to become accepted practice for electric vehicles. The Cleveland Machine Screw Company of Cleveland, Ohio made electric cars only in 1899 and 1900 and some 100 were exported to Europe, the British importer being C. Eagle-Bott of Norfolk Street, the Strand, London. Many of the Cleveland car features reappeared in the Waverley.

CORD

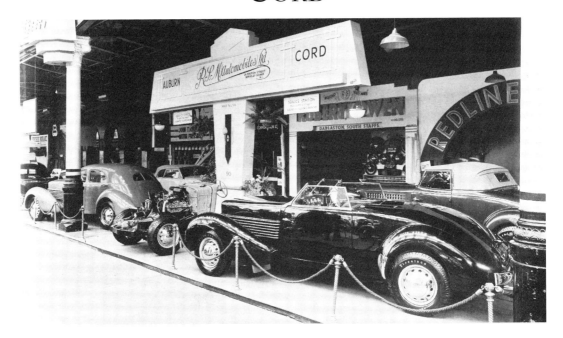

Above: The scene is the London Motor Show at Olympia in October 1936 where the Cord appeared for the first time and attracted a lot of attention. The instrument panel was described in *The Autocar* as of "very European type." Beyond the black 812 phaeton are a show chassis and a Beverley Custom four-door sedan. Rear, right is an Auburn 852 supercharged speedster. R.S.M. Automobiles in London was the distributor for Cord and Auburn.

Popeye.

Above: How *The Autocar* magazine's artist F. Gordon Crosby reacted to the new Cord at the 1936 London Motor Show.

Above: Although not registered until 1938 (in Southport, Lancashire) this Cord Sportsman convertible Model 812 cannot date from later than August 1937 when the company ceased production.

CROWN MAGNETIC

Left: A 1920 example of an ephemeral make from Wilkes-Barre, Pennsylvania, where the Crown Magnetic was itself only a renamed Owen Magnetic with the "magnetic" part being the Entz electro-magnetic transmission. The idca was to sell the chassis in England with English bodies, but very few were completed.

DODGE

Above: One wonders how a Dodge of the first full year of the company's production, 1915, found its way to Edinburgh, though this picture is post–1920 as proved by the license disc attached to the windshield upright. License discs were introduced in 1921 and are still the British tax receipt to show that the annual license duty has been paid.

Did the proud owner also construct the landaulette body on top of the touring car which was the only Dodge offered in 1915?

Left and right: Toward the end of the war Dodge had been providing ambulances for the European allies, but in 1918 a panel-side delivery and a screen-side truck also appeared. Here they are in England.

Above: A chauffeur poses with this 1921 Dodge fitted with an English landaulette body. Sidelamps were necessary in England, but this car also has a pair of oil lamps mounted flanking the windshield.

Left and right: Two British creations on the Dodge 116-inch commercial wheelbase. They both look a bit funereal except for the bow tie of Mr. Lee in the first photograph and the rear-entrance foot-step—which would not have been needed if the rear passenger were horizontal—in the second. It must be a station bus. The second body is by Arnold & Comben, Coachbuilders, of Farnham in Surrey.

Top: Seen here outside the clubhouse at Brooklands in Surrey is a 25 h.p. Dodge Senior Sedan. It was the car used by *The Autocar* magazine for a road test in May 1936 and was summed up as "a comfortable, easily handled big car, equipment in the English Style and overdrive transmission." *Bottom:* This Dodge Six was assembled at Mortlake Road, Kew, west of London, in 1937.

DURANT

Top and bottom: W. C. Durant had formed General Motors in 1908 but was forced to resign in 1910. He took control for a second time in 1915, resigning again in 1920. In 1921 Durant Motors was born, but after three good years the path was downhill.

At top, outside Mrs. Hood's guest house, a party is departing for a motor car outing. Below is a car kept by a stone from rolling backwards. The slope seems slight so one hopes the car's brakes were functional. Both are circa 1922.

Top and bottom: The top picture (both are from 1923/4) shows a family in the Scottish or Welsh hills having managed to lose seven of the eleven people with the car in the bottom picture.

DURYEA

Opposite, top and opposite, bottom, left and right: The "Locomotives on Highways Act" of 1896 allowed cars to be used in Britain for the first time without each one being preceded by a man on foot. The new "Motor Car Club" organized a rally of cars from London to Brighton on November 14. It was stated that four Duryea cars had come from Springfield, Massachusetts, for sale in England with two of them entered in the run.

Contemporary press coverage reports sightings of a Duryea car during the run, which was on a Saturday. The cars did not return to London until Monday as Sunday was respected as a day of rest. However a few of the cars were run on

Sunday and *The Autocar* reported: "Most of them were driven at reasonable speed but the Duryea was let loose—rushed about in an absurdly dangerous manner at almost twice the maximum allowed by law and it is a wonder no accidents resulted, as the traffic, both pedestrian and vehicular, was at its height at the time." Duryea was often reported in the British press in the early years of the last century.

E.M.F.

Above: Built in Detroit, Michigan, by Messrs. Everitt, Metzger and Flanders from 1908 to 1912 was the E.M.F. Model 30 with four cylinders and 30 h.p. This is a 1912 two-seat roadster.

Opposite: An Essex advertisement that appeared in *Autocar* in 1920.

ESSEX

THE ESSEX.

The most efficient standard stock car made.

LIVELINESS   POWER

TWO-PASSENGER ROADSTER.

ECONOMY   SILENCE

ESSEX SALOON SEDAN.

ESSEX MOTORS, Detroit, U.S.A.

Distributors for Great Britain and Ireland—

SHAW AND KILBURN, LTD., Wardour Street, London.
MORRIS GARAGES, LTD., Oxford.
GROSVENOR GARAGE, LTD., Bournemouth.
CASTLE MOTOR CO., LTD., Kidderminster and Birmingham.
PYTCHLEY AUTOCAR CO., LTD., Northampton.
W. WATSON AND CO., Liverpool.
RIPPON BROS., Huddersfield, Bradford, and Leeds.

UNITED AUTOMOBILE SERVICES, LTD., Bishop Auckland and Roya
    Buildings, Bigg Market, Newcastle-on-Tyne.
BOYCOTT AND CO., LTD., Norwich.
J. BOULD, LTD., Cardiff.
BRISTOL WAGON AND CARRIAGE WORKS CO., LTD., Bristol.
JOHN CROALL AND SONS, LTD., Edinburgh and Glasgow.
SPENCE AND JOHNSTONE, LTD., Belfast.
DUBLIN MOTOR CO., LTD., Dublin and Cork.

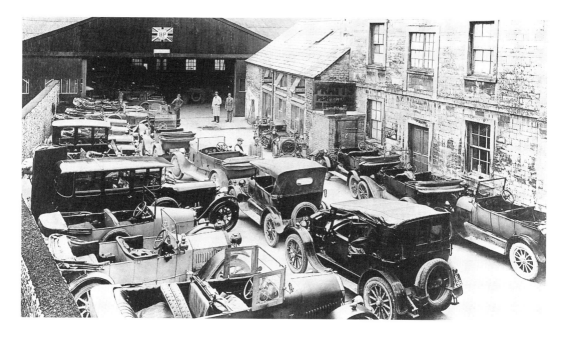

Above: This garage in Circencester, Gloucestershire, today has its yard roofed over. From bottom left are a Humber, a Hupmobile, left-hand drive French Cit-roën and a Sunbeam sedan with a Ford T Tudor sedan among the cars beyond it. The center line comprises an Essex, an unidentified car, a Vauxhall tourer and two Ford T's, one of which has left-hand drive.

On the right are a second unidentified car and two more Fords, the first of which is pre-war and the second has wire wheels. Beyond are several motorcycle combinations.

It would be a good rally today to produce such an interesting display.

Above: Only the registration, the sidelights, the tax disc and the city gent locate this photograph as England in 1927. This Essex is even parked on the wrong side of the road though this is not illegal in Britain.

Opposite, bottom: This picture may date from 1924 by which time the Essex in the center would have been British assembled. "The Travellers Rest" may look like any ordinary pub, but at this time it operated under the auspices of the "People's Refreshment Houses Association" which ensured that non-alcoholic beverages and refreshments were available and that alcohol was not externally advertised. The Association also required that bedrooms be available.

The First World War period two-seater Morris at left has an unusual painted radiator and naval-style ventilators on the cowl. The Essex sedan was registered in Aberdeen (Scotland) and behind it is a two-seater Rover Eight of 1922 whose horizontal twin-cylinder engine was air-cooled with the heads protruding on either side of the hood.

Above: A 1928 Essex sedan and a Morris of similar date beyond it are on the fore-court of the Beaulieu Road Hotel in the middle of the New Forest, a few miles from Beaulieu village and today's National Motor Museum. It is another "People's Refreshment Houses Association" establishment.

Opposite, bottom and below: Essex sedans of 1928, 1929 and 1931. The last one has a fabric body made under the patents of Charles Weymann. By 1931 fabric bodies were almost outmoded. The design was rattle-free and lightweight but the leather-cloth type of surface was not glossy and not long-lasting.

Above: Leslie Hounsfield, who had been responsible for introducing the Trojan car and van to 1920s England, resigned from Trojan in 1930 and was on his own again when he used this 1930 Essex sedan to demonstrate his next invention. The "Trojan Ambulance Carrier" cost £37 and must have given the two patients on the roof an earnest desire for the driver to reach the hospital sooner while— please—driving slower! For a further £8 the unit could be assembled as an emergency tent to provide sleeping accommodation for four people (two up, two down). It did not catch on, but Hounsfield's invention of a folding camp-bed did catch on and many survive today including one in the author's house.

Opposite: The scene is the Brighton sea front where a locally registered 1931 Essex coupé is parked. Essex was one of the most popular American cars in Britain.

ESSEX TERRAPLANE

Above: Miss Violet Cordery, here in the passenger seat of a 1933 Essex Terraplane, had been well known at Brooklands since 1925 when she first won there in an Invicta.

The next year she broke the world 10,000 mile and 15,000 mile records at Monza (as one of a team of six drivers). She took further records, all in Invicta cars, and won the Dewar Trophy in 1926 and again in 1929 for that marque. She drove this Essex Terraplane car in the 1933 Scottish Automobile Club Rally and with N. Black and H. E. Symonds won the team prize.

This Terraplane has English body by R.E.A.L. Carriage Works, then of Ealing, West London.

Opposite, top: For the British this is an Essex Terraplane Light Six drop-head coupé. The owner is Lady Astor (née Nancy Langhorne of Virginia) who became Britain's first woman member of Parliament in 1919. The Astor seat was Cliveden sited high above the River Thames near Maidenhead in Berkshire. It is now possible to stay there as today the house is a hotel. The hub-caps are just marked "Terraplane 6" and the mascot is a griffin.

The car's annual road tax was only £17 for a full-size car when Britain was in the grip of a horsepower-based road tax system.

Above: When the Terraplane was announced in England at the Motor Show in October 1932 it was as an Essex marketed by Hudson-Essex Motors, so 1933 cars are Essexes.

The driver is B. A. Blackford and he is competing in the Junior Car Club Rally at Brooklands in July 1939, where he won the Test Hill Sweepstake and a two-lap handicap race. In the background can be seen a stretch of the banking on the left, and the Test Hill beyond the car roof. The Campbell Circuit, built in 1937, is marked by the white posts on the far right.

FLANDERS

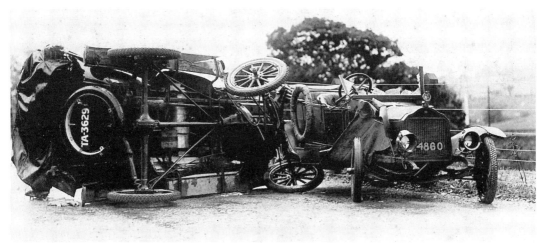

Top: A family sets out from Penrith between the Pennine Hills and the Lake District in England's north-west. One hopes the external passenger is not going too far! The car is a 1911 Flanders 20, which had been intended to compete in price with the Ford T but never could. The next year was to be Flanders' last before Studebaker took over. *Above:* July 2, 1922, was the day this Flanders expired while overturning the opposition in the form of an almost-brand-new Ford. Not all "improvements" to motor cars have been for the better, but one fears for the occupants behind that pre-safety-glass windscreen.

FORD

Above: One of the first Ford cars to be sold in Britain was this Model A of 1904. It cost £230 inclusive of the tonneau, the tubed tires and brass rails. The tonneau was the back seats with central rear access door; the assembly was detachable along the diagonal molding line. The engine was a flat twin of 8 h.p. located below the driving seat, where the starting-handle hole can be seen. The registration is from Perth in Scotland.

Above: On August 3, 1904, Bank Holiday Monday, a race meeting for touring cars was held at Bexhill on the Sussex coast. The course was a standing-start one kilometer ending on the brow of Galley Hill. In Class C, for cars costing £200 or under and carrying two persons, the Model A Ford of A. E. Culley beat the 7 h.p. Star of F. R. Goodwin. The Ford carries trade-plates and the Star has London registration.

Above: The Model N Ford of 15 h.p. was sold in some numbers in Britain. This scene is in the village of Norton-sub-Hamdon, Somerset, where the local doctor has stopped to talk to a patient. One hopes they did not all drive on the right in the village, which is close to Yeovil, but perhaps in 1906 there were no other cars in the village.

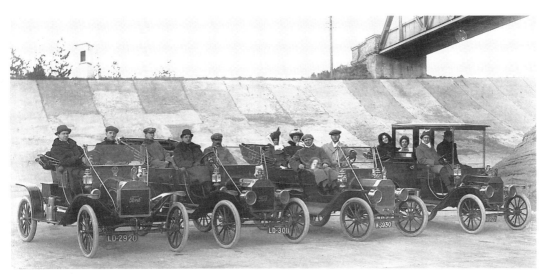

Top and bottom: The concrete-surfaced Brooklands track was finished in 1907. The top picture shows the junction of the Finishing Straight and the Members' Banking with the Members' (foot) Bridge above. Why four obviously new Model T Fords in touring use should be posing on the track at Brooklands is not obvious, but the cars all date from 1909 when Ford established London sales premises in Shaftesbury Avenue on October 1st. The first two cars and the landaulette have London registrations and right-hand drive while the Liverpool (K) registered tourer has left-hand drive. This latter car is shown again just round the corner to the right in the bottom photograph; the ladies' motoring scarves and veils are better seen. It may be Percival Perry, Henry Ford's English agent 1909–1922 and 1928–1948, who is at the wheel of the left-hand car.

Above: Said to have been pictured in May 1933 at Worth in Sussex is this 1910 Ford T. The body has only front doors on each side; another photograph (not shown here) shows the left side with the spare wheel rim stowed to the rear of the single front door. Both rows of seats are well upholstered, so how did the rear passengers gain access? Also what is the handbrake doing behind the driver's elbow?

Above: A very English car, but the windshield is original Ford. The conical headlights are electric and the oil side-lights have been electrified as a cable leads up from behind the fender. The steering wheel has been turned over, which looks more comfortable with the higher seating. The car has been fitted with detachable wheels with only three bolts to each as have the 1912 landaulette and 1913 tourer on the facing page.

Above: A landaulette ca. 1912 with a group showing mixed formality of dress. This is a Manchester-built right-hand-drive car.

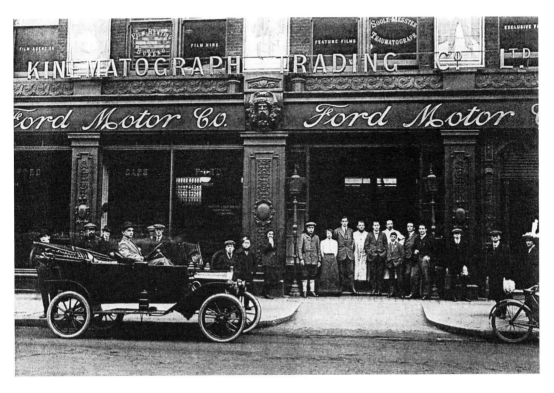

Above: The company's London showroom at 55 Shaftesbury Avenue in 1912.

Left: Nothing special about this 1913 tourer until one notes the wheels fitted with Warland detachable rims. The lighter cars in Britain before 1914 often had fixed rims, so the frequent punctures of the day made motoring sometimes a dirty activity.

The Warland Rim allowed for a spare tire to be carried already inflated on a rim. The rim also had a removable section allowing it to be expanded inside the tire, rather than having the tire stretched over the rim. The unit was then held onto the wheel by a metal ring and bolted in place.

Above: Another Ford with detachable wheels with three studs. The tourer body must be British.

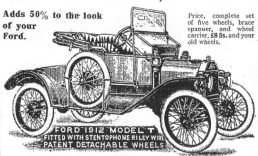
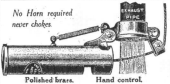

Above: A Ford advertisement that appeared in *The Autocar* in 1915.

STEPNEY COMBINATION WHEELS
For FORD CARS.

THE STEPNEY GROOVED TYRE

THE STEPNEY WHEEL

8·80×120

Price of STEPNEY Combination Wheel for Ford Car, size 30 x 3 and 30 x 3½ **£3 : 15 : 0**

Every Ford owner needs a Stepney Wheel. Thousands of Fords are already fitted with this most popular spare wheel.

Although the Ford Car is fitted with larger wheels on the back than the front, the Stepney Combination Wheel is suitable for both, **and avoids the necessity of carrying two spare wheels.**

Tyres on Fords are as liable to give trouble as on other cars. You cannot therefore be comfortable without a " Stepney."

You may have to repair a burst tyre on a miserable wet night, whereas with a "Stepney" you could be off again in a minute as if nothing had happened

THE STEPNEY SPARE MOTOR WHEEL, LTD.,
STEPNEY WORKS, LLANELLY.   168, Great Portland Street, LONDON W.

Above: A Stepney Wheel advertisement that appeared in *The Autocar* in 1915.

Right: A rather uninteresting landaulette with strengthened roof luggage battens, but all very English.

Above: Branscombe village is on the south coast of Devon between Exeter and Lyme Regis. A 1919 Surrey-registered Model T pickup waits outside a tea shop.

Opposite, bottom: Another group outing poses for the camera, so someone in this group in 1918 bought the photograph now in the author's collection. Beyond the 1918 Model T now fitted with accessory-shop radiator is a charabanc whose registration is ca. 1923, though the chassis is a pre-war Crossley. Seventeen passengers have squeezed in!

Above: Ford vans carrying signs for local businesses were a very common sight in the twenties. Here is one from the Sussex coast.

Above: An English-bodied landaulette with Southampton registration.

Above: This Model T Ford ambulance of 1926 vintage was made in Barnsley, Yorkshire, by Reynolds Brothers.

Above: This Ford AA chassis of 1929 was supplied—and probably bodied—by Reynolds Brothers (Barnsley) of Yorkshire. It has a Barnsley County Borough Council registration and yet was obviously supplied to a "cattle remover" in Royston, Hertfordshire, 150 miles south.

Above: This "Rose and Crown" hotel is at Thorney in Cambridgeshire about seven miles from Peterborough. Outside, in 1934, are a Hillman on the left and an Austin Heavy Twelve Four behind a Ford Deluxe V-8 Fordor sedan on the right. Ford V8s were first built in Europe in 1934, at Cork in Ireland, and from 1935 the Model 48 was produced at Dagenham in Essex.

Above: The owner of this 1939 Ford Deluxe Fordor sedan looks to be American, as does the driver's hat, but the collie dog is of Scottish descent and the background is English. The car was registered in April 1939 to Scammell Lorries of Watford in Hertfordshire, north of London. The year 1939 was the year that Henry Ford at last sanctioned the use of hydraulic brakes on his cars, but it was to be another ten years before Fords gained independent front suspension. Like the 1935 Auburn on page 9, the owners have done away with the maker's lights, mounting separate lamps on homemade brackets.

Opposite, bottom: A 1933 Ford Roadster, with headlights in the "go-faster" position but still laden with badges, competes on the seafront at Brighton in Sussex in the Brighton Speed Trials on September 21, 1934. At the far curb is parked a Riley, but number 108 is a different matter: The car has front and back axles from different sources and remains unidentified. The driver has his scarf flying in the manner that was the death of Isadora Duncan only a few years previously.

FRANKLIN

Above: Until its demise in 1934 the Franklin was America's principal air-cooled make, as the Volkswagen was in post–World War II Europe.

Here Mrs. H. V. Falk is in her V-windshield two-door sedan Franklin in Bognor Regis on the Sussex coast in 1924. It is a model 9-B of 1921–22.

Opposite: A 1913 coachbuilder's advertisement; a 1920 idea for updating an old Ford; and another coachbuilder's advertisement from 1922.

GARFORD

Above: From Elyria, Ohio, perhaps via European war service, this Garford chara-banc came to Croydon, Surrey. This group does not look overjoyed at the prospect of a day out as they pose for the camera. Perhaps they realize the photographer's intentions!

An excursion in those days was a memorable occasion. It was normal for a photographer to record all parties setting out and he would be present on the coach's return to sell copies of his pictures. At least one of the men on board posted one, and the card found its way into a postcard collection and eventually into the hands of a friend of the author.

GMC

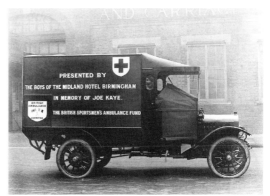

Above: Five thousand G.M.C. ambulances contributed to the British war effort and various persons and groups collected the money necessary. Here are four of them, all bodied by the Cunard Motor and Carriage Co. in Chiswick, west of London. Perhaps Mrs. Dresser inspected the back of hers (upper right) as the footstep is lowered. This vehicle also shows the roll-up Perspex windshield and the oil side-lamps have been electrified.

Above: The Anzac Motor Company traded from 78-82 Brompton Road, London, the road on which Harrods also fronts.

Anzac handled Oldsmobile, G.M.C. and Oakland cars, but it can only be the Oakland that was offered as a complete 6-cylinder, four-seater at an extremely cheap £300.

The GMC van outside is London-registered in 1915 but is a heavier vehicle than the ambulances shown on the previous page.

GRAHAM-PAIGE

Above: Would the driver of this very conservative-looking sedan of ca. 1929 really have attacked a hill "as a chance of a little harmless showing off," as the copy accompanying this advertisement suggests? Did this staid vehicle "bring new joy to motorists"? This ad appeared in *The Illustrated London News*, March 23, 1929.

GRANT

Above: The Grant Motor Company commenced in Detroit in 1913 with a two-seater sporting roadster with a 12 h.p. water-cooled engine that put it almost out of the cyclecar class, but at a time when cyclecars of similar appearance were in vogue it was difficult to escape. Cyclecars were popular for only a couple of years in America, but in Britain their popularity did not finish until after the Austin Seven was introduced in 1923.

This London-registered 1914 Grant with right-hand drive was marketed in England as the Whiting-Grant, sales being handled through Whiting of Euston Road, London. By 1916 the makers transferred to the manufacture of bigger cars, and production ceased in 1922.

HARLEY-DAVIDSON

Above: Englishmen did not normally chew cigars but perhaps this one thinks it is an image appropriate to his mount. A handwritten note on the photograph reads "O.H.T. & Hazel aged 7 weeks."

HUDSON

Right: Although registered in Perth, Scotland, with a 1908 number, this is surely a later Hudson Model 33 with a body by Bayleys of London that seems outdated. The English call this a shooting brake. While it could be used for collecting people and luggage from the station (thus as a station wagon) it was also used for carrying the beaters to and from the location of the shoot and also for bringing back the game shot.

Above: Another Hudson Model 33 of 1911 with English landaulette body giving the chauffeur a little extra rain protection. A Stepney spare rim is carried as the wheel rims are non-detachable.

Above, left and right: Both cars are 1935 Hudsons and both are bodied by Coachcraft of London. The Special Sports model had the wire wheels. The 117-inch chassis was lowered, the hood was given sloping louvers and the close-coupled body was very smart.

Right: This creation on a 1935 Hudson Eight is to the design of Captain Fitzmaurice by Lancefield Coach Works in West London. The full-width body seated four in the front (with one to the right of the driver) and three in the rear. Suitcases fitted in luggage lockers behind the front wheels; the luggage had to be removed and a panel slid aside to allow mechanical access to the

engine. Further luggage lockers were behind the rear wheels and tools were with the spare wheels in the tail. Floor compartments behind the doors allowed golf clubs, fishing rods etc. to be carried.

Above: The Hudson Terraplane stand at the London Motor Show in 1936. From the left are an Eight club sedan, a Terraplane sedan, a Coachcraft sports sedan (similar to the 1935 Hudson) and at far right a long-wheelbase Eight special club sedan.

Hudson Terraplanes sold well in Britain, and the company had a headquarters on the Great West Road west of London. Right-hand drives in all styles as well as chassis were available. It was a fast car in six-cylinder form and even more impressive as a straight eight.

Above: John Cobb was the last Brooklands lap recordholder (Brooklands did not restart after the Second World War). In 1938 he took the World Land Speed Record in his four-wheel-drive Railton at 350.2 m.p.h., and the next year raised it to 369.74 m.p.h., both at Bonneville, Utah.

John Cobb is seen here with his Hudson De Luxe club sedan for the English market in 1937.

HUPMOBILE

Left: A two-seater coupé on a 1911 Hupmobile in London. The high-mounted headlights were a Hupp characteristic until 1914.

Above: A standard-bodied 1913/14 Hupmobile in an English setting.

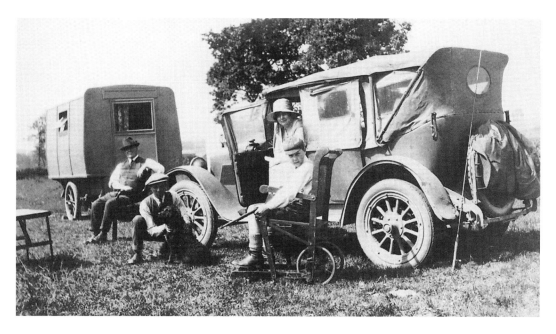

Above: A British family on holiday. The boy sits in a rickety wheelchair whose front caster wheels are really not suitable for grass. The boy holds a rifle; the father holds a dog. There are a fishing rod and a tent. The 1920 Hupmobile is also equipped to tow the camper.

Above, left and right: The body on left hand 1924 Hupmobile is similar to that by the same coachbuilder on a 1924 Chrysler earlier in this book.

Post Card

CORRESPONDENCE   ADDRESS

Owing to special circumstances we are selling a limited number of these elegant eight cylinder (27 h.p.) saloon cars at ridiculous prices. A trial will convince you that this is the chance of a lifetime. Silent, flexible, and fast, they add a new pleasure to driving.

INTERNATIONAL DISTRIBUTORS Ltd.
78, Brompton Road, S.W. 3.
Tel. KENSINGTON 9601

Above: The message on the back of the upper right postcard says it all in 1928. Britain was in a slump.

JEWETT

Above: The Jewett was made from 1922 to 1927 by the Paige-Detroit Motor Car Company; this is a Standard Touring of 1925.

KING

Above and left: Charles King drove the first gasoline-powered car on the streets of Detroit a few months earlier than Henry Ford's initial journey. He spent two years in Europe before starting his own company selling King cars from 1911. The company seems to have limped along until 1923 but Mr. King was out in 1912. There was good exporting during the good years. This English King cabriolet must date from 1914 as no cars would have been imported the next year due to the war.

From about 1905 the British had occasionally attached dolls, teddy bears or stuffed policemen to car fronts. The Rolls-Royce company combatted this unseemly behavior by having its Spirit of Ecstasy mascot designed in 1911.

Less well known is the stag's-head mascot which had been introduced as a badge for Hertfordshire County Automobile Club in 1908. This King was Hertfordshire registered.

The Delight of Every Owner
And the Envy of Friends.

EIGHT CYLINDER

Mass production on highly organised scientific lines has resulted in a car of infinite comfort and luxury, possessing ample speed and power, and including every mechanical refinement appreciated by motorists of experience and discrimination. No other car of the same price can compete with the "KING-Eight" in power, speed, comfort, or enduring service. The new KING Models are on view in our showrooms. Will you make an appointment for a trial run?

NOTE:

The "King" has a low-built chassis specially suitable for English Coachwork. Chassis Price, **£700.**

SALMONS & SONS

(Originators of All-Weather Bodies),
SOLE CONCESSIONNAIRES,
6-9, Upper St. Martin's Lane, W.C.2.
'Phones: GERRARD 3338 - - - NEWPORT PAGNELL 29.

PRICES:

"7-Seater Touring Car," **£820**; "4-Seater," with detachable wire wheels and one spare wheel, **£875**; "Sporting Speedster," with 5 detachable wire wheels and 5 tyres complete, **£875.**

Above: A 1919 King touring car with admiring onlookers.

KRIT

Top and bottom: The English landaulette body (bottom) fits well in spite of the factory front fenders being retained on this 1913 Krit while the tourer outside the Wingrove Hotel (top) retains its factory touring body. The Krit was made in Detroit from 1910 to 1915. The company specialized in exporting to Europe, so when war broke out in 1914 the company was fatally affected.

LA SALLE

Above: The La Salle marque was introduced by General Motors in 1927 as a downscale Cadillac rather than a higher class Buick, but here it shares its prestigious showrooms with Buick. Two La Salles are backed by five Buicks in Woods' Garage at the Holstein Hall in Weybridge, Surrey.

LITTLE

Right: Made in Flint, Michigan, only in 1912 and 1913 as a William C. Durant production, the Little competed with Durant's other new marque, Chevrolet. It was Chevrolet that made it. The windshield springing from the bulkhead is unusual as there is wind-deflecting bodywork behind it.

LOCOMOBILE

Above: The Hon. Charles Rolls (later the famous partner of Henry Royce) bought this 5 h.p. Locomobile in 1901. In March and again in June 1902 he used it when the Automobile Club of Great Britain and Ireland (ACGBI) demonstrated the motorcar to police chief constables and county councillors.

The car is seen here on July 6, 1901, at the start of the hillclimb of Dashwood Hill near High Wycombe in Buckinghamshire on the road from London to Oxford. Press reports do not record Charles Rolls' presence and the Locomobile is being driving by A. E. Ginder, who may subsequently have bought the car as he is shown driving it in 1902 complete now with a condenser.

Opposite: Locomobile advertisements of 1902 and 1903.

Above: The Marquess of Salisbury, British conservative Prime Minister, is a passenger in his 1900 Locomobile outside his country home, Hatfield House, Hertfordshire, in 1902. It was as Robert Cecil that he became a member of Parliament in 1853 and prime minister for the first time in 1885. A Nobel Prize winner, he retired in 1902. The car is driven by his son, Lord Robert Cecil, who became an M.P. in 1903 and also was awarded the Nobel Peace Prize in 1937. Lord Salisbury's family home, Hatfield House in Hertfordshire, was the seat of the Cecil family back to Robert Cecil, the first Earl of Salisbury, who was Secretary of State to Queen Elizabeth I in 1596.

Above: Two members of Parliament pose in a courtyard of the House of Commons. Sir John Dixon Poynder is in the 1902 Locomobile and Major John Seely is alongside.

Both of these Locomobiles are fitted with Clarkson steam condensers at the front. It was illegal to emit visible water vapor on the road.

WHAT IS IT?

THIS illustration depicts one of the many attempts by inventors to relieve the—to them—ungraceful lines of the modern car. The formation of the shield in front very successfully prevents the throwing up of dust, as during the passage of the car the rush of air is deflected on either side, instead of being swirled about between the

bottom of the car and the road. It also lends itself to being used as a steam-condenser, and is fitted at the same time with a sliding window, to protect the occupants of the car from driving rain and high winds. The Texas Motor Company, 31, Museum Street, London, are responsible for this somewhat radical departure from the general acceptation of what should be a motor car's " lines of beauty."

Left and below: Press reports of 1902 (left) and 1905 (below).

A MAGISTRATE'S MOTORS.

WHILE so much prejudice continues to be displayed amongst magistrates against the use of the automobile, it is interesting to take note of cases in which magistrates themselves are automobilists. Such a one is Colonel R. P. Davis, J.P., of Walton-on-the-Naze, Essex, who has had three cars in succession, all of which he still retains. The vehicles in question consist of two 10 h.p. Locomobile touring cars and a 16-22 h.p. De Diétrich coupé. It is satisfactory to observe that Colonel Davis is eminently contented with his possessions, and, writing to Messrs. Jarrott and Letts on the subject, he states : " I like them *all* very much, but, of course, Mrs.

Davis prefers the De Diétrich, as it is so handy in all weathers."

MAIBOHM

The Wonderful Six Cylinder Twenty

BRIEF SPECIFICATION:

Engine—Six-cylinder (R.A.C. Rating 23.5.)
Valves—Overhead.   Lubrication—Forced feed.
Fuel Supply—Autovac.   Ignition—Magneto.
Dynamo Lighting.   Self starter.
Brakes—Both act on rear wheels.
Back Ax'e—Full floating.
Rear Springs—Underslung 52 inches long.
Timken Bearings.   Tyres—815 × 105.
Hood—One Man Type.   Equipment—Spare Rim, Tool
Kit, Jack, Pump, Tyre Repair Outfit, Side Curtains, etc.
Wire Wheels—£25 extra.

THE FOLLOWING TERRITORY IS AVAILABLE TO APPROVED AGENTS:

Scotland   Ireland (except Ulster)   Oxford   Cambridge
Northampton   Gloucester   Dorset
Somerset   Devon   Cornwall   Hereford
Monmouth   Nottingham   Lincoln
Rutland   Durham   Northumberland   Cumberland
Huntingdon   East Kent   South Wales

English Coupe Body £795
Sports Model £695   Standard Touring Model £595

SOUTHGATE, LTD.,
SOLE CONCESSIONNAIRES FOR G. B. & I.,
Showrooms: **19-21, Heddon Street, Regent Street, London, W.1.**
Telegrams: "Maibohms, Reg, London."
'Phone: Regent 3321.

Above: Maibohm Motors Co. of Racine, Wisconsin, and then Sandusky, Ohio, assembled a four-cylinder car and then a six for which British agents are sought in this 1919 advertisement. They may not have found any, as the 1920s Motor Car Index lists the makers as the British agents and perhaps few were sold in the period 1920-1921.

MAIFLOWER

Above: In the heady first days of peace after World War I there was a shortage of cars. Two army captains, M. Price and A. I. Flower, used their demobilization grants to market modernized Ford T's in Gloucester. The rear of the chassis was replaced and all lowered. A Frontenac head, detachable disc wheels and four forward speeds must have improved the original. The bodies were British. This Maiflower is made from an earlier left-hand drive original but has 1920 Somerset registration.

MARMON

Left: This 1927 Marmon sedan must be the Little Eight four-door with fabric-covered roof. It was photographed in east Surrey.

MARQUETTE

Above: Some amused locals inspect the underside of a fallen Marquette on the road between Aberystwyth and Devil's Bridge in West Wales. Marquette was introduced by Buick as a new smaller line for 1930. The stock market crash that year doomed such a venture, so it was made for only the one year.

Right: A British army officer and a Boy Scout display a 1930 Marquette.

MAXWELL

Above: Maxwell-Briscoe was formed at Tarrytown, New York, in 1904, so this 1905 Maxwell Model H is an early arrival in London for this photograph. It had a flat twin engine of 4" × 4" and the make did well in many Glidden Tours.

Above: Three Model 25 Maxwells of the period 1916–1919. One tourer (*top left*) has wartime lamp black-outs and the other (*bottom*) has oil sidelights as has the landaulette (*top right*) with acetylene headlamps.

Opposite, bottom: A British landaulette on a 1910 Maxwell four-cylinder 30 h.p.

METZ

Above: This Metz with English two-seater body is probably a 1912. In 1908 and 1909 the Metz had been available for purchase on the Metz Plan whereby the car could be bought in $25 packages for self-assembly over a period.

MITCHELL

Above: Just after World War I this Mitchell was made with a six-cylinder engine. It was the start of the company's decline to bankruptcy in 1923.

MOON

Above: With all its sidescreens up this looks quite British, but it is a 1924 Moon tourer with registration ?T-6217, otherwise much as it must have left the factory at St. Louis, Missouri.

Opposite, bottom: Taken at the Botallack tin mine, St. Just in Penrith, Cornwall, is this photograph of a ca. 1910 Mitchell 30 h.p. In the scene note that the laborers on both ends of the group have their trousers tied with string, a normal custom for agricultural workers at the time and perhaps for tin-miners too.

NATIONAL

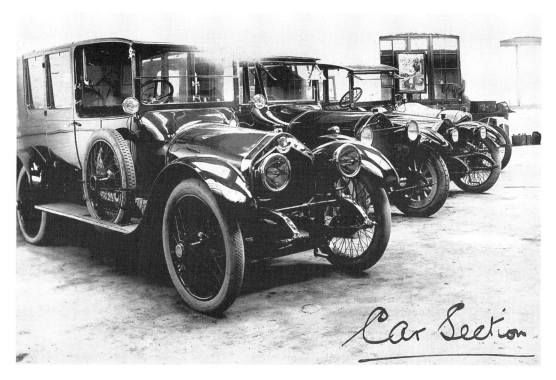

Above: The three English cars (first, third and fourth from left) are Crossleys made in Manchester, all 1914 models. Between them, second from left, is a 1918 National Highway Six sedan. The National was made in Indianapolis from 1900 to 1924. These cars are parked in the Martin Motorcycle Works at Woking in Surrey where the Martinsyde motorcycle was made in the early 1920s.

NOMA

OAKLAND

Above: Outside the Victoria and Albert Museum in Knightsbridge, London, is this ugly-duckling body on a 1918/19 Oakland chassis. It is perhaps a staggered two-seater with forward-placed jump seat. Without the extra side window we would call it a coupélet. One hopes the reason for the egg-shaped rear is that it houses the spare wheel.

Right: The scene is London toward the end of the war to judge by the blacked-out street lamp. The car is an Oakland of 1917 with a four-seat sedan body by H. J. Mulliner & Co. of London. The driver has an armchair seat adjustable for reach while the passenger seat folds to allow access for the rear passengers. The central gear and brake levers allowed the driver easy access on the other side.

Opposite, bottom: The Noma was an "assembled" car from the Lower East Side of New York, built from 1919 to 1923 with Continental or Beaver six-cylinder engines. This is a 1921 Noma, one of only a few hundred made. Nomas had diver's-helmet fenders extending very low at front and back. Step plates allowed the elimination of running boards, and the bodywork was aluminum panelled over laminated wood. That a car so rare at home ever came to Britain is remarkable.

Above: Until 1919-1920, cars in Britain had their sidelights mostly cowl-mounted. Here Grosvenor Carriage Co. of London has made a "doctor's coupé with dickey" (rumble seat) on a 1918 Oakland chassis.

Above, left and right: A Cornwall-registered Oakland of 1918 (*left*) working as a taxi has all pre-war acetylene and oil lighting while the similar 1919 tourer (*right*) has American electric headlights and English electric sidelights.

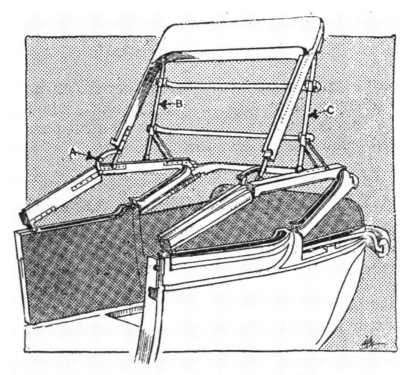

The framework of the head of the Cole coupé-cabriolet body. A is a special hinge; B and C are telescopic and spring-loaded tubes by the assistance of which the head can be raised or lowered single-handed.

Top left, right, and above: By 1919 British coachbuilders were getting back into their stride. These two Oakland convertible coupés both have considerable presence and class to eclipse the 1918 offering.

Whether or not the coachbuilder was William Cole & Sons of Hammersmith, the folding mechanism would have been as shown in this *Autocar* drawing of 1915.

THE TOWN HALL, HORSHAM. 7.

Opposite and above: In 1924 Oakland, of Pontiac, Michigan, introduced a new L-head engine, front-wheel brakes, and lacquer cellulose paint. The resultant Oakland Greater Six (*opposite*) is seen in 1926 outside the Horsham, Sussex, Old Town Hall. The other Sussex-registered sedan is from 1927.

OLDSMOBILE

A YEAR'S EXPERIENCE WITH AN OLDSMOBILE:

BY CAPTAIN SIR R. K. ARBUTHNOT, BART., R.N.

THE following account gives the cost of running an Oldsmobile car for a year. The vehicle was purchased in August, 1902, being among the first to take the road in England, and it was immediately started off

IMPROVED MUDGUARDS.

on a tour to Strathpeffer and back from Eastbourne (see THE CAR of December 3rd, 1902). A very careful record of expenditure and mileage has been kept, from which it appears that 6,530 miles have been run during the year. The car has been in continuous use, and employed as follows :—

August, 1902 to November, 1902.— Touring to Strathpeffer and back from Eastbourne (2,400).

December, 1902 to March, 1903.— Daily use in London.

April, 1903.— London to Holyhead.

April, 1903.— Round G.B. course to Waterford.

April, 1903.— Milford Haven to Eastbourne in two days, 340 miles, with one puncture. one chain, and two slow speed clutch adjustments.

End of April, 1903. — Week - end trip, London to Welbeck and back, for the Eliminating Trials.

May, 1903.—Daily use in London.

June to August, 1903.—Daily use in Portsmouth, with long week-end runs.

The car has only once failed to reach its destination, and that was through the accumulators giving out four miles from home. During the tour to Scotland we paid thirteen visits and stayed at fourteen hotels, and were only late once through voluntarily stopping a night in Inverness to have the valves ground in. The chain wore out in 5,000 miles,

but the first 3,000 were run without a chain case, which should double the life of a chain. The crypto gears had to be rebushed after the tour to Scotland. This was partly due to defective design of oiling arrangements, and partly to inexperience and want of attention on my part. All front wheel cones have been changed—worn—but this is a very simple matter. The pinion on front end of cam shaft has been turned round, to equalise the wear, and pins of valve working rollers renewed.

Expenses : —

Outlay.	£	s.	d.
Motor (with hood, back seat, and mudguards)	200	0	0
Dress and clothing	19	19	5½
Accessories and additions	36	9	3½
Insurance (CAR 1902 policy)	13	11	0
Sundries	1	7	6
Four accidents to carriage (each under £5)	15	8	9
Licence	2	2	0
	£285	17	0

Running Expenses for 6,530 Miles.

	£	s.	d.
Petrol	15	1	11
Tyres	25	7	0
Spares, repairs, overhauls	30	16	0
Dry batteries	2	12	6 (First tour.)
Lubricating oil	1	15	10
Cleaning	1	19	2
		77	12	5
Wages to man for eight months	33	11	1

SIR R. K. ARBUTHNOT'S OLDSMOBILE AFTER RUNNING 6,530 MILES.

Stables and room, eight months	37	15	8
		71	6	9
	£148	19	2

£77 12s. 5d. is just over 2¾d. per mile.
£71 6s. 9d. is just over 2⅝d. per mile.

The £285 17s. is practically all outlay. The same car, with many improvements, is, I see, now selling for £150. The dress item is large, as we started off on a long tour at once. Repairs to carriage were accidents, through side-slipping once, and crumpling up near front wheel. This was due to careless driving. Also, through twice cracking front part of body, again carelessness, and no fault of any part of motor. It will be seen that practically half the running expenses are for wages of a man and for stabling. Stabling in London is expensive. My driver was a young bluejacket, who was invalided out of the Navy; he knew nothing about mechanic's work, but soon learned to drive and run the car in town and keep it in order.

The first four months, when on our tour, my wife and I managed the car entirely by ourselves, except for carriage cleaning. Anyone having a stable or a shed even, and a gardener or a boy, could be free of the " wages and stabling " item. It is absolutely unnecessary to keep a mechanic to run an Oldsmobile. The item " repairs and overhauls " was largely due to the wearing of the gears, but I understand that in this year's pattern, these have been very greatly improved, and practically run in oil. The petrol works out at just over a halfpenny a mile.

We repaired punctures ourselves for the first six months, but have since found it is much more satisfactory to send them to the Imperial Tyre and Rubber Company, Brooke Street, Holborn, for repair. The car never moves far from home without carrying a spare tyre. A new one is easily put on in twenty minutes. " Diamond " single tube tyres have been used throughout, and the car is still running on her second set. In the stable the car always stands on four wooden trestles to keep her off the tyres. Punctures have averaged one a month.

I recommend the following :—A hood and a back seat, the former is most useful for coats, rugs, spare petrol, etc., when down, and the latter for the driver if one is kept, or for giving a lift to a third or even a fourth passenger. Peto and Radford's G 40 accumulators. Leather hanging mudguards, as shown in photograph, they keep engine wonderfully clean. Wheel mudguards, as shown, with patent leather wings to front ones. Chain case, or " boot " as it is called in America. Front wheels taken off, lubricated and adjusted monthly. Rear wheels taken off, and rear rollers taken out and cleaned and tubes washed out in wake of rollers monthly, and also after any long muddy run. A piece of patent leather 7 in. by 4 in., with a hole in it for the cam shaft, and hung just in front of the commutator is a very good fitting, as it allows plenty of oil to be used on the worm which works the cam shaft, and keeps this oil off the commutator ; not that the oil itself matters much, but the dirt, grit, and dust the oil collects do, very much indeed.

As a runabout, or for a medical man, the Oldsmobile cannot, in my opinion, be beaten. It is so handy, so light, so easy to get in and out of, and so easily stopped and started that I can only say, after the thorough trial I have given it, that if I wanted another two-seated car, which I do not because mine is still running so well, I should certainly buy a 1903 Oldsmobile.

At a recent meeting of the Wiltshire County Council it was decided to purchase a motor-car for the use of the county surveyor.

Opposite and above: An account from Sir R. K. Arbuthnot of Frome in Somerset of his satisfaction with his Oldsmobile in 1903.

Right: The Stanley Cycling Club, which had promoted bicycle shows since 1876, put on a motor show at Earls Court, London, in January 1903.

Above: Mr. C. D. Rose of Hardwick House, Reading, was a member of the Jockey Club, a breeder of racehorses and a member of Parliament. He is seen here (*left*) in 1904 with his 16 h.p. four-cylinder Argyll car from Glasgow in Scotland. His son (*center*) has a 10 h.p. four-cylinder Panhard et Levassor from Paris, France, while Mrs. Rose (*right*) "drives regularly" her Oldsmobile.

Above: Ranson E. Olds formed Oldsmobile in 1900 but a factory fire in 1901 delayed the marketing. Mr. Olds left his company in early 1904 just as this curved-dash single-cylinder Oldsmobile might have been coming to England to join the London & North Western Railway.

EXPERIENCES WITH AN OLDSMOBILE.

A MONGST the many satisfied owners of Oldsmobile cars is Mr. Arnold White, who since January last has steadily used one of these little vehicles every day in the course of his business around London. He has not had the least trouble with the engine, with batteries or ignition, inlet valves, or any part of the motor, and his tyre troubles were entirely due to the use of sharp flakes of flint by the Hampstead Borough Council, and cannot be attributed to the type of tyre supplied by the Oldsmobile Company. With the chain he had some slight trouble, which he ascribes to the inexperience of his man in starting the vehicle suddenly on a steep hill at too great a speed.

As an example of the work which Mr. White gets out of this little car we may take his experiences during a recent week, when having gained confidence in the car and found that he could absolutely rely upon it to keep appointments

It should be noted that Mr. White obtained these satisfactory results although a novice, and the man he employed was a groom and also had no experience of motor vehicles. The Oldsmobile has therefore been tested under very trying circumstances, and its excellent behaviour in the hands of novices is a very striking proof of its simplicity and reliability.

MR. ARNOLD WHITE ON HIS OLDSMOBILE.

at a distance punctually to the minute, he determined to submit it to a test. His first proceeding was to lend it to a county council candidate, and for nearly twelve hours it was kept going up and down the steep hills of Hampstead. This was a severe test, and nothing went wrong. A few days later he was obliged to go to Portsmouth, and he travelled in the car over Hindhead to Whale Island and back to his residence without the slightest hitch of any kind. One-third of the ascent of Hindhead was taken at the top speed, and he averaged about fourteen miles an hour on the way back. On arrival at his home the car was as sound as when it started, and an overhauling showed that everything was in good order.

With regard to the expense, Mr. White finds that it costs him less than fly and cab hire, while it saves him twenty-five minutes in every hour that he is travelling. It has also greatly increased his radius of activity while giving him more time for brain work. Mr. White believes his Oldsmobile to be the best car in the world at the price (£150). It is, he says, more silent, more trustworthy, and more efficient than any car of its size that he has met.

Above: Another satisfied Oldsmobile customer reports in April 1904.

Above, left: Reliability was an important selling-point for early automobiles. *Right:* Another early Oldsmobile advertisement, this one from 1904.

Above: By the following year, 1905, there was a four-seat "light tonneau" with 7 h.p. single-cylinder engine still located under the seats. The lady's pudding-basin hat was probably the height of fashion as her car sets out from Newport in Monmouthshire.

Above: A 1915/16 Model 42 Oldsmobile roadster of 30 h.p. and 192 cubic inches capacity with its standard American body. It is posed here in front of the Victoria and Albert Museum in London's Knightsbridge. While the top has obviously been raised, one would suspect that it is newly arrived in England (see also several Oaklands photographed in the same location).

Above: The big horseshoe radiator dates this Oldsmobile 30-B tourer to 1924. A pleasant scene on a country run.

Above: This 1927 Oldsmobile Model 30-E sedan was first registered in London in early 1928.

Above: The Oldsmobile Six, L-Series touring sedan of 1936.

OVERLAND

The 20-25 h.p.
OVERLAND
Price complete as shown,
ready for the road . . £250

Above: This is an advertisement card sent by Overland agents Macfarlane Bros. in Perth, Scotland, to Mr. Bussel, cycle and motor agent in nearby Pitlochry: "22.7.1912. Sir as your hiring season is now on you will be doing a good business."

Opposite and above: The Overland landaulette of 1918 (*opposite, top*) carries the Union Jack and white ribbons which demonstrate a car being used to carry a bride to church and the married couple away to the reception. The tourer from a year later (*opposite, bottom*) has a toy monkey sitting on the radiator and oil side-lights to show a certain unease with the new-fangled electricity. The advertisement (*above*) shows a van.

Above: Overland's London service station about 1912 with a tourer and a light van posed outside. The bottom line on the painted wall behind might well read "Willys-Overland Limited." Unfortunately the original glass negative from which this picture is printed is broken, so the reason for the spectator interest around the entrance is lost.

Left: Apart from my informing the reader that South Woodford is in Essex, this charming piece of 1920 advertising can stand on its own.

Above: Parked in front of Romsey Abbey (near Southampton) in August 1926 is a 1920 Overland.

Above: Two Gloucester-registered Overlands performing a fuel-consumption test with Royal Automobile Club observers on board. A new company, Willys-Overland-Crossley, was formed in 1920 and Overlands were assembled in a factory at Heaton Chapel, Manchester, by Crossley Motors and bodied in England. There was also a 13.9 h.p. Morris Oxford-engined Overland to reduce the liability to British horse-power tax, so these two may have been testing smaller engines.

PACKARD

Above: The registration plate of the Packard is LF-338? which is of London County Council in 1912. However, this car was surely made during the war and bodied in England afterwards in the "all-weather" style with V-windshield, which was built in large numbers at the time by William Cole & Sons, a short-lived coachbuilder from Hammersmith. The hood, fenders, lamps, horn and battery box are all Packard. The Houk wheels were almost unknown in England.

Above: What the British call a cabriolet body on a Packard ca. 1924.

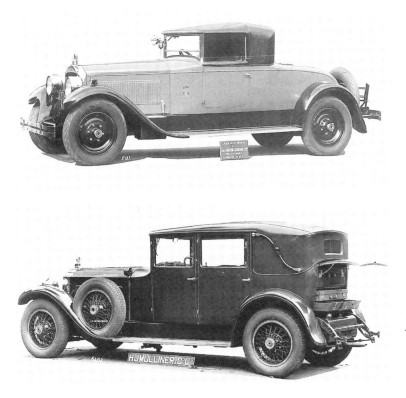

Middle: Retaining its American headlamps is this smart two-seater with rumble-seat by Carlton Carriage Co. of London. *Bottom:* Coachbuilders H. J. Mulliner were established in London in 1900. This Packard Model 443 Eight of 1928 has a Weymann patent fabric body and a neat concealed luggage compartment. The Weymann plate appears at the bottom between the doors, but as on all British coachwork, the builder's signature is out of sight on the door step-plates.

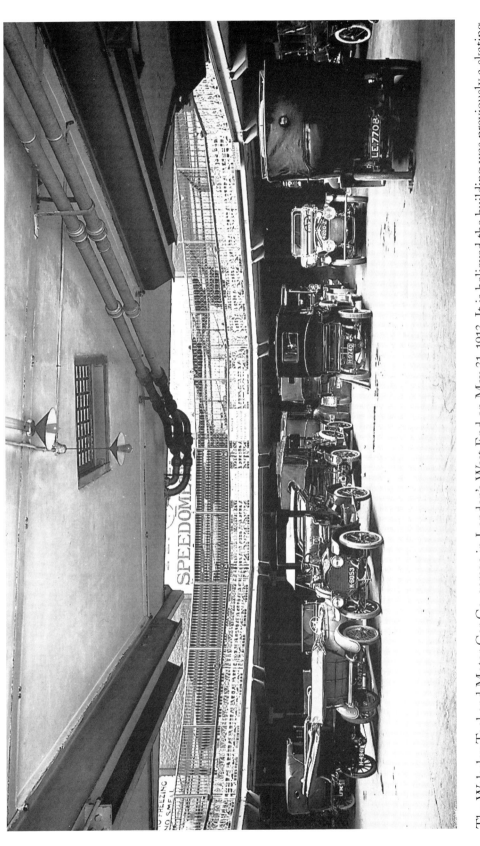

The Wolseley Tool and Motor Car Co. garage in London's West End on May 31, 1913. It is believed the building was previously a skating rink. Among the customers' cars are two Packards. K-6053 is a Liverpool registration while 4200-Z is a left-hand drive car, probably with an American body and registered in France.

Above: This 1928 Packard has managed to make it to Britain in original factory specification.

Most British cars have always been smaller than American ones. The seated gent reminds the writer of the lovely description given by the late John Bolster in his book *The Upper Crust* defining a gentleman's car. It was one where the running board was long enough to accommodate two bottoms, two glasses and a bottle. This Packard was thus a gentleman's car!

Above: Although bearing a triangular badge, this is still a Packard runabout ca. 1928. The multi-color sheep might mean the photograph was taken in mainland Europe.

Above: This Packard Standard Eight, ca. 1930 but with 1932 registration, carries chrome-plated radiator shutters, RAC. AA and Brooklands badges, and diplomatic plate (C.D.) but presumably no heater; the chauffeur has a rug ready for the passengers.

FREESTONE & WEBB LTD.

Above: This is a Super Eight Packard long-wheelbase limousine with eight cylinder engine. It is a guess that this car, registered in Middlesex but photographed near Winchester in Hampshire and parked outside a church, would have been used in the funeral trade.

Opposite, bottom: Freestone & Webb (formed in 1923 in Willesden, London) streamlined coachwork in their "razor-edge" style on a 1938 Packard Eight chassis No. 502281.

PAIGE

Above: In 1915 Paige-Detroit introduced a six cylinder car so this must be one of the last fours.

PAIGE-JEWETT

Above: This is a Paige-Jewett of ca. 1923 setting out on a chauffeured outing from Ilfracombe in Devon. The picture is on a postcard sent to London on June 24, 1929, which reports, "We are having a topping time."

Opposite, bottom: Although this 1921 car might have been sold as a Jewett in its native land, it is a Paige in Britain, the cheaper Jewett name coming as a Paige-Jewett in 1923. What a pretty thatched cottage!

Forethought made possible this Exceptional Price

Forethought reduced the price of PAIGE–JEWETT Motor Cars £100 in view of the impending legislation removing the import duty. Buyers can now share in the benefits of this forethought by taking advantage of the special introductory offer of PAIGE–JEWETT Motor Cars. Forethought built the original PAIGE–JEWETT Motor Car— that is so economical in operation, both on petrol and oil, and will accelerate on top gear from 5 to 25 miles per hour in 7 seconds.

Forethought made possible this quality *Six* cylinder motor-car at the price of a good "*Four.*"

This same forethought built a motor car of such exceptional qualities as to suit the motorist who wanted a car of simplified engineering construction, yet incorporating all the benefits contained in a car of much higher price.

It was this forethought in motor car construction that made 115,000 buyers choose the PAIGE-JEWETT in the two years and two months since the first PAIGE-JEWETT Motor Car was offered for sale.

If your district allotment has not already been exhausted, use forethought and purchase a PAIGE–JEWETT Motor Car with the duty removed from the price and all the good engineering features retained. Enjoy the pleasure of your motor car now instead of waiting for the law to take effect in August.

PAIGE–JEWETT Motor Cars can now be had at the new price of £295, which means the duty charge is borne by us.

YOUR OLD CAR TAKEN IN PART PAYMENT.
DEFERRED PAYMENTS ARRANGED.

Specification

Engine — 6 cylinder, $3\frac{1}{4} \times 5$ · lubricated by high pressure oiling to main and connecting rod bearings ; two - unit electrical starting and lighting, thermostatically controlled ; automatic spark advance ; Paige - Timken axles. Chassis—extra heavy 6 in channel steel frame ; 3 speeds forward and reverse ; special Paige dry plate clutch : special alloy steel springs ; all steel universal joints ; forced feed chassis lubrication. Cooling — forced water circulation by centrifugal pump. Brakes—large brake drums 14 in. in diameter, furnishing a brake service of 18-21 pounds per square inch, automatically adjusting themselves to the stress demanded. Leather upholstery Colour— Moleskin Grey

These are only a few of the special exclusive engineering features found on a Paige-Jewett.

NO FURTHER REDUCTION AUGUST 1st !

*Motor Car Dealers who are interested in taking up the
Agency should communicate with Head Office.*

PAIGE-JEWETT CARS, Ltd., 16-17, PALL MALL, S.W.1.

PAIGE-JEWETT

Above: A 1924 Paige-Jewett ad from *Autocar* magazine.

PEERLESS

Above: It is a pity there is no information about the circumstances in which this picture of three top-quality cars from three countries was taken. A London-registered Peerless tourer is on the left dwarfing a ca. 1910 Silver Ghost Rolls-Royce with tourer body by Barker of London. The Rushmore headlamps and bumper bar are very American but the registration is French. On the right is a Panhard et Levassor, again ca. 1910 and also with French registration. The squared ends of the roof rack would indicate Labourdette of Paris as the coachbuilder and the big leather box on the roof contains spare tires.

Both the Peerless and the Panhard have British AA badges, and the left-side opera lamp of the Panhard has a green glass rectangle as was the law in France at the time to show on which side traffic should pass.

Above: A four-cylinder Peerless of about 1910 with Liverpool registration, American windshield and Rushmore headlights.

The fenders are domed, and that must be a footstep with a box under it pretending to be a chain cover as all Peerlesses had shaft drive. A Peerless had been brought to Europe in 1903 when Louis P. Mooers drove one in the 1902 Gordon Bennett Race on the Athy Circuit in Ireland. He did not finish.

PIERCE-ARROW

PLYMOUTH

Above, top and bottom: Two 1937 model Plymouth P2 sedans but with no details of their locations.

Opposite, bottom: Another American truck to help the British war effort was this Pierce-Arrow seen outside the London shop of Alfred Herbert machine tool makers.

RAILTON

Above: Noel Macklin had responsibility for the Invicta, designing in 1925 a car with a big unstressed American-style engine (by Meadows) in a car of British tradition with good road-holding. Reid Railton had designed land speed record cars. The two men set up in the ex–Invicta works in Cobham, Surrey, in 1933 to make a hybrid based on the Terraplane 8 chassis (and on the Hudson 8 from 1934), lowered and with stiffer suspension. Classic British bodywork with riveted hood, as on the Invicta and the Silver Ghost Rolls-Royce from 1907, was used.

The 1934 Railton sports saloon is bodied by Abbey Coachworks.

Above: A Railton Coachcraft sedan of 1936.

Opposite: This 1935 convertible is a Fairmile Series One by Coachcraft bought new by the author's doctor's father in Croydon. It is seen here with wartime blackout lamp covers and white-painted fenders.

Above: Rippon was Britain's oldest firm of coachbuilders, based at Huddersfield in Yorkshire. It was also a top-quality builder as these pictures of a well-fitted Rippon sedan body on a 1937 Railton show. The car was the property of Colonel Rippon, who won many prizes at Concours d'Elégance and competitive events before the war.

R.C.H.

Above, top and bottom: Robert C. Hupp resigned from Hupmobile in 1911 to build the R.C.H., which lasted from 1912 to 1915. Here are two English-bodied cars of 1912/13 of which, surprisingly, the second (*bottom*) has had non-detachable wheel-rims fitted. Surely a retrograde step.

REGAL

Opposite, top and bottom, and above: The Regal had an "underslung" chassis which passed beneath the car's axles. The family seen at opposite top surround a 20 h.p. two-seater roadster. The four-seater at the bottom is a Model SF, and the two-seater above is the Model H. It is a card posted in Honiton, Somerset, to Sergeant Cordland at the town's police station. All the cars are 1912 or 1913.

Regals exported to England were sold by Seabrook of Great Eastern Street, London and known as R.M.C.s or Seabrook-R.M.C.s.

REO

Above: Major Cotesworth on his new 16 h.p. Reo ca. 1905.

Above: Reo buildings, Broad Sanctuary, Westminster, S.W.

Above: Small 10 h.p. Reo.

Right: 1907 16 h.p. Reo, front view.

Above: The factory bodied car that obtained 798 marks out of a possible 800 for reliability in the Scottish Trials in August 1906. Mr. H. Gordon Sharpe is at the wheel.

Above: Mr. F. Graham Sharp, who made the record Top Gear Run from London to Brighton and back, is at the wheel of the Scottish Trials car on February 28, 1907.

Above and below: This 16 h.p. Reo was delivered to this lady by Reo Motors Ltd. of Broad Sanctuary, Westminster, London in January 1907 and was the first of its type. At the time it was reported that "quite a number are on order."

Above: The 1908 Reo two-seater.

Above, left and right: These two very tired little buses were, one hopes, no longer in service. They are photographed at Reigate Bus Depot in Surrey and are both Surrey registered. The Reo, at left, was registered (PD) in 1924 and the Chevrolet (PK) is a 1929 Type LQ 1-ton chassis.

Opposite: 1924 Reo advertisement in *The Autocar* magazine.

Above, top and bottom: Reo was in difficulties in the early thirties and in 1936 announced that it would continue exclusively with commercial vehicles. At top is a Reo horse-box built by Strachans to Hammond's patent at Rutland Garage in Newmarket, the horse-breeding and racing center in Suffolk. The lower photograph shows a Reo bus with "26 seat Hackney Carriage" license in the livery of F. R. Wadd near Leicester and built by Bracebridge Motor Works in Lincoln. Both are late 1920s models.

RITZ

Above: A young man "putting on the Ritz"! The popularity of the cyclecar in the United States was very short, lasting only from 1913 to 1915. In Europe it began a little earlier and lasted into the early twenties. The Ritz cyclecar was actually made in Sharon, Pennsylvania. It is 1915-registered and had a four-cylinder engine of 10 h.p. and sold at £120.

AT THE SHOW.

"WHAT MY HUSBAND AND I REALLY REQUIRE IS A *SMALL* TWO-SEATED CAR—ONE WE COULD
DRIVE OURSELVES."

Above: The tiny Ritz could well have filled the bill for the corpulent couple in this
cartoon from *The Car*, 1904.

ROAMER

Top: The Roamer from Kalamazoo was an "assembled" car but a quality one, so how did a British coachbuilder contrive to create such a dull slab-sided body? The Rolls-Royce-copy radiator and hood do not make an easy shape for the coachbuilder to follow, but he should have done better than this.

Bottom: The car above it has cantilever rear springs whereas this chassis shows semi-elliptics. The photograph is taken with a time exposure in a residential road; the sheet would have been kept moving to give a neutral background for use in catalogs or magazine illustrations. In this case one assumes the photographer was commissioned to show only the front half.

RUGBY

Above: W. C. Durant's Durant empire included the Star Four, designed to be a competitor for the Ford T. It was sold outside the United States as the Rugby to avoid conflict with the English Wolverhampton-built Star cars. This one is from 1926 and has had pressed steel wheels and low-pressure tires fitted, which might have improved the ride but did nothing for its looks.

SAXON

Above: The Saxon commenced in 1913 and by 1916 was the eighth-largest United States manufacturer. This is a 1914 car with right-hand drive.

STANLEY

Above: A 1905 Stanley 8 h.p. Model CX runabout with the front seat-back raised and a big water condenser below it. These condensers were necessary to comply with British law.

Above: The 1907 Stanley Model F 20 h.p.

Above: Third from the left is a Stanley four-seater on "trade-plates." The car is probably a 1908 model and the venue is the Hut Hotel at Wisley in Surrey, which would be demolished for road-widening after World War II.

From the left, the other cars are: a two-cylinder French Darracq, an oval-radiator two-cylinder Riley, the Stanley, and a four-cylinder Talbot. After unidentified cars and motor-cycles are a Humber (LB-5885, second from right) and another unidentified car.

Above: The Model H-5 Gentleman's Speedy Roadster. There are marks showing that a windscreen has been fitted but removed again.

Above: This Stanley ca. 1911 has the dullest of English bodies. The importers/coachbuilders were Galloways of Gateshead, who traded in the motor business as Stanley Steam Car Ltd.

STUDEBAKER

Above: This Studebaker bears Fife (SP) registration, so it's not surprising that the young man at the wheel is wearing his Scottish Tam O'Shanter and a sporran.

Above: It would be good to imagine a kind-hearted Cardiff civilian taking wounded soldiers for a run in his motor car during the First World War. It is a 1913 Studebaker Model 25.

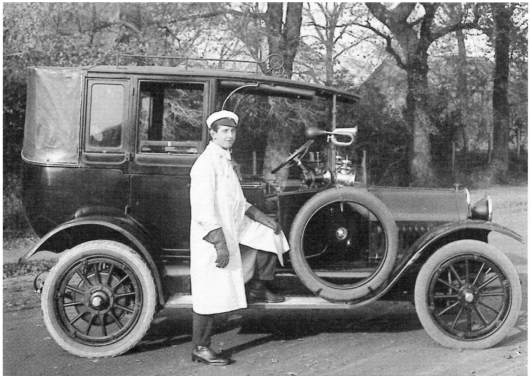

Top and bottom: English landaulettes of 1913 and 1914 on Studebaker 25 chassis.

Above: The location for this Studebaker is the Brooklands motor course in Surrey with the hangars in the background.

Above: The chassis is ca. 1915, but Sturt-Goatcher of Farnham in Surrey must have completed the car in 1919 as no such work would have been done during the war. The outcome is a leather-topped doctor's coupé on a Studebaker SD-4.

Opposite: A 1915 Studebaker advertisement from *The Autocar* magazine.

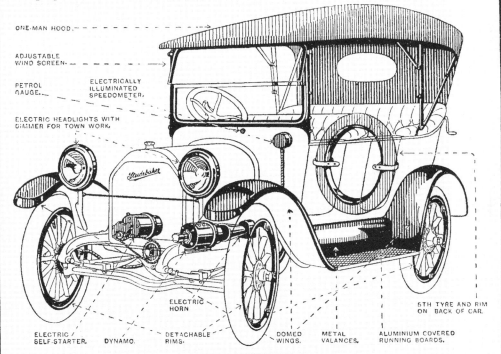

Above: A would-be member of Parliament must have thought that his ca. 1922 Studebaker sedan might help his chances. While the body is British, the headlamps are American.

Left: A Studebaker from 1935 pictured during World War II, with black-out headlights and white-painted all round (a Railton is similarly shown). *Right:* A 1937 Studebaker President Sedan. The "V" badge on the grill is that of the Veteran Motorist's Association. A number was let into the base of the badge to indicate how many years the member had driven without an accident.

Opposite, bottom: Stutz hood louvers were horizontal but this is an English body. The doors cannot have been easy to open with the hinges not vertical, and the fashionable low roof would have made it feel claustrophobic by today's standards. This may be the 1929 London Motor Show car registered DV 32.

STUTZ

Above: A 1928 Stutz with body by Arthur Mulliner of Northampton using Weymann patents.

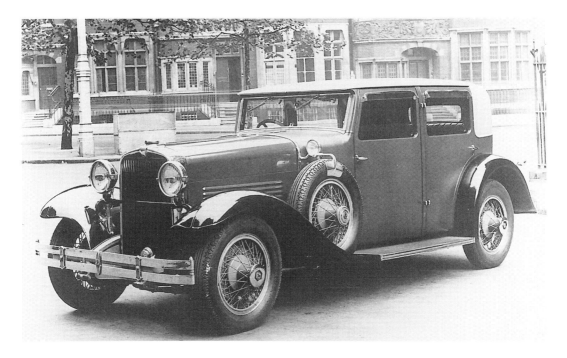

Above: This 1929 Stutz Blackhawk six-cylinder car is bodied by Weymann and is seen here before its black leather-cloth roof covering was fitted.

Above: Having driven this eight-cylinder supercharged Stutz at the 1929 Le Mans race with George Eyston as co-driver, R. Watney drove the car, entered by Colonel Warwick Wright, the British importer, in the 1929 Tourist Trophy Race. The T.T. had given up the Isle of Man course after 1922 and for 1929 it was to be on the Ards Circuit near Belfast in Northern Ireland. The Stutz must have been too big a car for the course and did not finish.

Above: Warwick Wright in London were English agents for the Stutz. Here on their stand at the London Motor Show in October 1934 is the SV16 with 5,277 c.c. eight-cylinder engine and body by John Charles, painted black with green moldings and upholstery.

Right: John Charles & Co. built bodies only from 1932 to 1934, when Ranalah (G. B.) started in south-west London. This is a John Charles saloon on a 1934 Stutz.

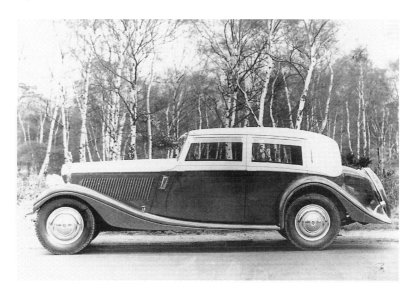

TERRAPLANE

Above: First seen at the October 1937 London Motor Show and described in *The Autocar* magazine as "resembling the Hudson" is this Terraplane sedan of 1938 with six-cylinder engine.

VIM

WALKER

Above: Several London shops had fleets of electric delivery vehicles supplied by the Walker Vehicle Co. of Chicago, Ill. This one in Selfridge's livery was registered in 1919.

Opposite: The Vim Motor Truck Company of Philadelphia had a short run from 1914 to 1926, but this one at least got to England.

WHITE

Above: The White steam car stand at the Stanley Show, London in February 1903. The show was promoted by the Stanley Cycling Club, which had nothing to do with the American Stanley car.

Opposite, above: A White of 1903-04 with the standard body. Mr. and Mrs. Seymour Hicks are in it.

Above: Sutton is in Surrey, and the old wooden building was the carriage-works of W. Leeding. This is a 1903/4 White. The rear face-to-face seats fold away to create a two-seat car with luggage platform. The front wheels carry beaded-edge tires as one would expect, but solids are fitted at the rear.

Above: BH is a Buckinghamshire registration. Here is Mr. H. R. de Salis at Ivy Lodge, Iver Heath, Bucks, in his 10 h.p. White tonneau. The White was first registered on February 9, 1905, and replaced his 1902 4 h.p. Locomobile two-seater-plus-spider of 1902. It was itself replaced by a Model E White (BH-826) in 1907.

Above: A White advertisement from 1905.

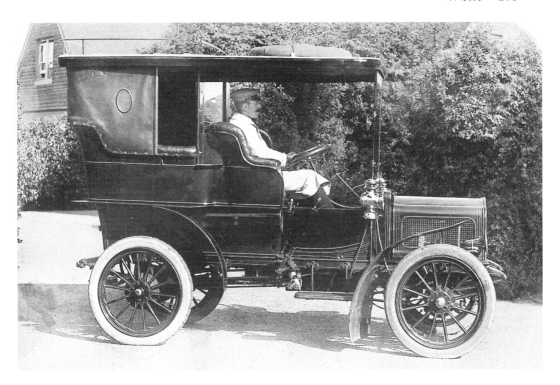

Above: A canopy-top touring White Model E of 1905 with partial side-curtains erected.

Above: The Model F White touring of 1906. The windshield and the forward-opening door lead one to the opinion that the body is English. Nothing malicious is intended in pointing out the enormous tool-box under the running board!

Above and opposite, top: On the reverse of this photograph is written:

August 21 1909
Lady Evans' car nearly raised by the combined efforts of chauffeur, Dr. Packer, Stephen, some farm boys. Figures at left, Lady Brocklebank pointing, Lady Evans, tip of Miss Evans' motor bonnet, Frank Reiss—a stranger visiting in the neighbourhood who afterwards sent these photographs, taken by his aunt, to Lady Brocklebank.

Opposite, bottom: Presumably in use during World War I is this 1909 steam engined White.

August 21. 1909.
Lady Evans' car nearly raised
by the combined efforts of chauffeur,
Dr Parker, Stephen, some farm
boys.
Figures to left - Lady Brocklebank
pointing, Lady Evans,
tip of Miss Evans' motor bonnet,
Frank Reiss - a stranger visiting
in the neighbourhood who afterwards
sent these photographs. Taken by
his aunt, to Lady Brocklebank

2

£1.50

The incomparable

White Steam Car

is the most flexible car on the road.
Try it, and test its flexibility.

15 h.p. White Landaulette.

15 h.p. White Chassis, £385 complete.
40 h.p. White Chassis, £700 complete.

The White Company,

36, Kingly Street, Regent Street, London, W.

Above: A White advertisement of 1909.

Above: Although it carries London registration of 1908, this White is petrol-engined so must be a 1910 model. Not only is this a magnificent car but the body is surely detachable too. There would normally have been rings fitted on the roof. A set of pulleys in the garage allowed the top part of the body to be lifted off leaving an open touring car for the summer.

Right: The cabriolet body on this 20/30 White with engine starting and lighting as well as magneto ignition was made by coachbuilders Cann of Camden Town, London, who bodied all English Whites in 1913.

The cars were often offered as White-Colemans, incorporating the name of Frederick Coleman, who was the British agent and a great publicist for Whites.

This particular car has been fitted with Warland detachable wheel rims.

WICHITA

Above: All the way from Wichita Falls in Texas came this Wichita truck to help England's war effort.

WILLYS-KNIGHT

Above: The Knight sleeve valve engine was the invention of C. Y. Knight, English-born but living in Wisconsin in 1905. His first customer was Daimler in England, but Willys-Knight used the engine from its start in 1914 and a Knight-engined car was still being offered in 1931. This sedan is of 1925 but may have come to England in 1931 to judge by its registration.

WINTON

Top, left and right, and above: In February 1905 Major General Sir Henry and Lady Colville went to the London Motor Show at Olympia and bought this two-cylinder 20 h.p. Winton Touring. Their home was "Lightwater," at Bagshot in Surrey, and his car's "P" registration is Surrey too.

Exactly a year later Sir Henry Colville exchanged his 20 h.p. Winton for a new Model "K" Winton (*bottom*) with four cylinders and 5.8 litres but still only two forward speeds. The road-spring shape is a particular feature of Wintons in 1905 and 1906.

Above: Photographed in Sussex is a 1906 Winton touring with canopy. The single headlamp was made by Polkey.

Opposite bottom and above: In 1907 Mill Court, Cholsey near Wallingford, Berkshire, was the home of Mr. G. L. Venables, who had bought a 3-h.p. De Dion Bouton in 1900 and then a Weston steam car into which he put a Cadillac engine. His stable in 1907 comprised three Wintons and a Cadillac. The Cadillac rearentrance tonneau and the two-cylinder Winton date from 1904 and the fourcylinder touring and four-cylinder limousine are both 1905. On the left is the Winton with Surrey. Top also shown opposite. Next to it is a four-cylinder Winton limousine and then a two-cylinder Winton touring and the Cadillac on the right.

Appendix A:
Tax Discs

Below appear a selection of tax discs of the twenties and thirties as fitted to the windshield or special holders of every road-licensed car. The disc is the receipt that demonstrates the car is taxed for the period shown. The tax disc system came into force in 1921 and could be bought for the calendar year or a quarter year. These discs are still used today and are now valid for twelve months from the first of any month. The colored strip changes shape or color for each year.

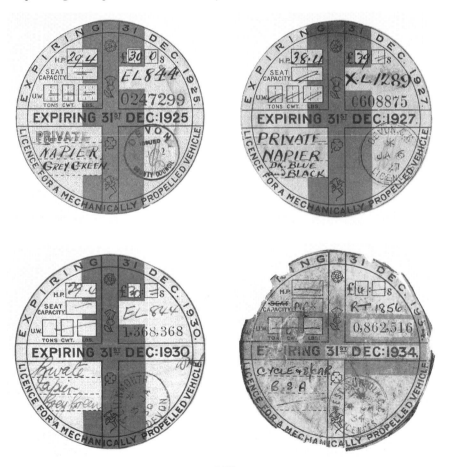

APPENDIX B:
REGISTRATION LETTER CODES

In the following list, letters after a place name indicate the status of the Licensing Authority: (B)—Borough; (C or C)—County or City; (LB)—Large Borough; (BC)—Burgh Council.

A	London	BH	Buckinghamshire
AA	Hampshire	BI	Monaghan
AB	Worcestershire	BJ	Suffolk (East)
AC	Warwickshire	BK	Portsmouth (B)
AD	Gloucestershire	BL	Berkshire
AE	Bristol (B)	BM	Bedfordshire
AF	Cornwall	BN	Bolton (B)
AG	Ayrshire	BO	Cardiff (B)
AH	Norfolk	BP	Sussex (West)
AI	Meath	BR	Sunderland (B)
AJ	Yorkshire (NR)	BS	Orkney
AK	Bradford (B)	BT	Yorkshire (ER)
AL	Nottinghamshire	BU	Oldham (B)
AM	Wiltshire	BV	Blackburn (B)
AN	London	BW	Oxfordshire
AO	Cumberland	BX	Carmarthenshire
AP	Sussex (East)	BY	London
AR	Hertfordshire	BZ	Down
AS	Nairnshire	C	Yorkshire (WR)
AT	Kingston-upon-Hull (B)	CA	Denbighshire
AU	Nottingham (B)	CB	Blackburn (B)
AV	Aberdeenshire	CC	Caernarvonshire
AW	Salop	CD	Brighton (B)
AX	Monmouthshire	CE	Cambridgeshire
AY	Leicestershire	CF	Suffolk (West)
AZ	Belfast (B)	CG	Hampshire
B	Lancashire	CH	Derby (B)
BA	Salford (B)	CI	Laoighis
BB	Newcastle-upon-Tyne (B)	CJ	Herefordshire
BC	Leicester (B)	CK	Preston (B)
BD	Northamptonshire	CL	Norwich (B)
BE	Lincolnshire (Lindsey)	CM	Birkenhead (B)
BF	Staffordshire	CN	Gateshead (B)
BG	Birkenhead (B)	CO	Plymouth (B)

CP	Halifax (B)	EU	Breconshire
CR	Southampton (B)	EV	Essex
CS	Ayrshire	EW	Huntingdonshire
CT	Lincolnshire (Kesteven)	EX	Great Yarmouth (B)
CU	South Shields (B)	EY	Anglesey
CV	Cornwall	EZ	Belfast (B)
CW	Burnley (B)	F	Essex
CX	Huddersfield (B)	FA	Burton-on-Trent (B)
CY	Swansea (B)	FB	Bath (B)
CZ	Belfast (B)	FC	Oxford (B)
D	Kent	FD	Dudley (B)
DA	Wolverhampton (B)	FE	Lincoln (B)
DB	Stockport (B)	FF	Merionethshire
DC	Middlesbrough (B)	FG	Fife
DD	Gloucestershire	FH	Gloucester (B)
DE	Pembrokeshire	FI	Tipperary (NR)
DF	Gloucestershire	FJ	Exeter (B)
DG	Gloucestershire	FK	Worcester (B)
DH	Walsall (B)	FL	Huntingdon
DI	Roscommon	FM	Chester (B)
DJ	St. Helens (B)	FN	Canterbury (B)
DK	Rochdale (B)	FO	Radnorshire
DL	Isle of Wight	FP	Rutland
DM	Flintshire	FR	Blackpool (B)
DN	York (B)	FS	Edinburgh (C or C)
DO	Lincolnshire (Holland)	FT	Tynemouth (B)
DP	Reading (B)	FU	Lincolnshire (Lindsey)
DR	Plymouth (B)	FV	Blackpool (B)
DS	Peeblesshire	FW	Lincolnshire (Lindsey)
DT	Doncaster (B)	FX	Dorset
DU	Coventry (B)	FY	Southport (B)
DV	Devon	FZ	Belfast (B)
DW	Newport (Mon) (B)	G	Glasgow (C or C)
DX	Ipswich (B)	GA	Glasgow (C or C)
DY	Hastings (B)	GB	Glasgow (C or C)
DZ	Antrim	GC	London
E	Staffordshire	GD	Glasgow (C or C)
EA	West Bromwich (B)	GE	Glasgow (C or C)
EB	Cambridge	GF	London
EC	Westmorland	GG	Glasgow (C or C)
ED	Warrington (B)	GH	London
EE	Grimsby (B)	GJ	London
EF	West Hartlepool (B)	GK	London
EG	Huntingdon	GL	Bath (B)
EH	Stoke-on-Trent (B)	GM	Motherwell & Wishaw (LB)
EI	Sligo	GN	London
EJ	Cardiganshire	GO	London
EK	Wigan (B)	GP	London
EL	Bournemouth (B)	GR	Sunderland (B)
EM	Bootle (B)	GS	Perthshire
EN	Bury (B)	GT	London
EO	Barrow-in-Furness (B)	GU	London
EP	Montgomeryshire	GV	Suffolk (West)
ER	Cambridgeshire	GW	London
ES	Perthshire	GX	London
ET	Rotherham (B)	GY	London

GZ	Belfast (B)	JH	Hertfordshire
H	London	JI	Tyrone
HA	Warley (B)	JJ	London
HB	Merthyr Tydfil (B)	JK	Eastbourne (B)
HC	Eastbourne (B)	JL	Lincolnshire (Holland)
HD	Dewsbury (B)	JM	Westmorland
HE	Barnsley (B)	JN	Southend (B)
HF	Wallasey (B)	JO	Oxford (B)
HG	Burnley (B)	JP	Wigan (B)
HH	Carlisle (B)	JR	Northumberland
HI	Tipperary (SR)	JS	Ross & Cromarty
HJ	Southend (B)	JT	Dorset
HK	Essex	JU	Leicestershire
HL	Wakefield (B)	JV	Grimsby (B)
HM	London	JW	Wolverhampton (B)
HN	Darlington (B)	JX	Halifax (B)
HO	Hampshire	JY	Plymouth (B)
HP	Coventry (B)	JZ	Down
HR	Wiltshire	K	Liverpool (B)
HS	Renfrewshire	KA	Liverpool (B)
HT	Bristol (B)	KB	Liverpool (B)
HU	Bristol (B)	KC	Liverpool (B)
HV	London	KD	Liverpool (B)
HW	Bristol (B)	KE	Kent
HX	London	KF	Liverpool (B)
HY	Bristol (B)	KG	Cardiff (B)
HZ	Tyrone	KH	Kingston-upon-Hull (B)
IA	Antrim	KI	Waterford
IB	Armagh	KJ	Kent
IC	Carlow	KK	Kent
ID	Cavan	KL	Kent
IE	Clare	KM	Kent
IF	Cork (County)	KN	Kent
IH	Donegal	KO	Kent
IJ	Down	KP	Kent
IK	City and County of Dublin	KR	Kent
IL	Fermanagh	KS	Roxburghshire
IM	Galway	KT	Kent
IN	Kerry	KU	Bradford (B)
IO	Kildare	KV	Coventry (B)
IP	Kilkenny	KW	Bradford (B)
IR	Offaly	KX	Buckinghamshire
IT	Leitrim	KY	Bradford (B)
IU	Limerick	KZ	Antrim
IW	Londonderry	L	Glamorgan
IX	Longford	LA	London
IY	Louth	LB	London
IZ	Mayo	LC	London
J	Durham (County)	LD	London
JA	Stockport (B)	LE	London
JB	Berkshire	LF	London
JC	Caernarvonshire	LG	Cheshire
JD	London	LH	London
JE	Cambridge	LI	Westmeath
JF	Leicester (B)	LJ	Bournemouth (B)
JG	Canterbury (B)	LK	London

LL	London
LM	London
LN	London
LO	London
LP	London
LR	London
LS	Selkirkshire
LT	London
LU	London
LV	Liverpool (B)
LW	London
LX	London
LY	London
LZ	Armagh
M	Cheshire
MA	Cheshire
MB	Cheshire
MC	London
MD	London
ME	London
MF	London
MG	London
MH	London
MI	Wexford
MJ	Bedfordshire
MK	London
ML	London
MM	London
MN	Isle of Man
MO	Berkshire
MP	London
MR	Wiltshire
MS	Stirlingshire
MT	London
MU	London
MV	London
MW	Wiltshire
MX	London
MY	London
MX	Belfast (B)
N	Manchester (B)
NA	Manchester (B)
NB	Manchester (B)
NC	Manchester (B)
ND	Manchester (B)
NE	Manchester (B)
NF	Manchester (B)
NG	Norfolk
NH	Northampton (B)
NI	Wicklow
NJ	Sussex (East)
NK	Hertfordshire
NL	Northumberland
NM	Bedfordshire
NN	Nottinghamshire
NO	Essex

NP	Worcestershire
NR	Leicestershire
NS	Sutherland
NT	Salop
NU	Derbyshire
NV	Northamptonshire
NW	Leeds (B)
NX	Warwickshire
NY	Glamorgan
NZ	Londonderry
O	Birmingham (B)
OA	Birmingham (B)
OB	Birmingham (B)
OC	Birmingham (B)
OD	Devon
OE	Birmingham (B)
OF	Birmingham (B)
OG	Birmingham (B)
OH	Birmingham (B)
OI	Belfast (B)
OJ	Birmingham (B)
OK	Birmingham (B)
OL	Birmingham (B)
OM	Birmingham (B)
ON	Birmingham (B)
OO	Essex
OP	Birmingham (B)
OR	Hampshire
OS	Wigtownshire
OT	Hampshire
OU	Hampshire
OV	Birmingham (B)
OW	Southampton (B)
OX	Birmingham (B)
OY	London
OZ	Belfast (B)
P	Surrey
PA	Surrey
PB	Surrey
PC	Surrey
PD	Surrey
PE	Surrey
PF	Surrey
PG	Surrey
PH	Surrey
PI	Cork (B)
PJ	Surrey
PK	Surrey
PL	Surrey
PM	Sussex (East)
PN	Sussex (East)
PO	Sussex (West)
PP	Buckinghamshire
PR	Dorset
PS	Shetland (Zetland)
PT	Durham (County)

PU	Essex		
PV	Ipswich (B)		
PW	Norfolk		
PX	Sussex (West)		
PY	Yorkshire (NR)		
PZ	Belfast (B)		
QA	QE	QJ	QN
QB	QF	QK	QP
QC	QG	QL	QQ
QD	QH	QM	QS

London: for vehicles temporarily imported from abroad

R	Derbyshire
RA	Derbyshire
RB	Derbyshire
RC	Derby (B)
RD	Reading (B)
RE	Staffordshire
RF	Staffordshire
RG	Aberdeen (C or C)
RH	Kingston-upon-Hull (B)
RI	City and County of Dublin
RJ	Salford (B)
RK	London
RL	Cornwall
RM	Cumberland
RN	Preston (B)
RO	Hertfordshire
RP	Northamptonshire
RR	Nottinghamshire
RS	Aberdeen (C or C)
RT	Suffolk (East)
RU	Bournemouth (B)
RV	Portsmouth (B)
RW	Coventry (B)
RX	Berkshire
RY	Leicester (B)
RZ	Antrim
S	Edinburgh (C or C)
SA	Aberdeen
SB	Argyll
SC	Edinburgh (C or C)
SD	Ayrshire
SE	Banffshire
SF	Edinburgh (C or C)
SG	Edinburgh (C or C)
SH	Berwickshire
SJ	Bute
SK	Caithness
SL	Clackmannanshire
SM	Dumfriesshire
SN	Dunbartonshire
SO	Moray
SP	Fife
SR	Angus
SS	East Lothian

ST	Inverness-shire
SU	Kincardineshire
SV	Kinross-shire
SW	Kircudbrightshire
SX	West Lothian
SY	Midlothian
SZ	Down
T	Devon
TA	Devon
TB	Lancashire
TC	Lancashire
TD	Lancashire
TE	Lancashire
TF	Lancashire
TG	Glamorgan
TH	Carmarthenshire
TI	Limerick (B)
TJ	Lancashire
TK	Dorset
TL	Lincolnshire (Kesteven)
TM	Bedfordshire
TN	Newcastle-upon-Tyne (B)
TO	Nottingham (B)
TP	Portsmouth (B)
TR	Southampton (B)
TS	Dundee (C or C)
TT	Devon
TU	Cheshire
TV	Nottingham (B)
TW	Essex
TX	Glamorgan
TY	Northumberland
TZ	Belfast (B)
U	Leeds (B)
UA	Leeds (B)
UB	Leeds (B)
UC	London
UD	Oxfordshire
UE	Warwickshire
UF	Brighton (B)
UG	Leeds (B)
UH	Cardiff (B)
UI	Londonderry (B)
UJ	Salop
UK	Wolverhampton (B)
UL	London
UM	Leeds (B)
UN	Denbighshire
UO	Devon
UP	Durham (County)
UR	Hertfordshire
US	Glasgow (C or C)
UT	Leicestershire
UU	London
UV	London
UW	London

UX	Salop
UY	Worcestershire
UZ	Belfast (B)
V	Lanarkshire
VA	Lanarkshire
VB	London
VC	Coventry (B)
VD	Lanarkshire
VE	Cambridgeshire
VF	Norfolk
VG	Norwich (B)
VH	Huddersfield (B)
VJ	Herefordshire
VK	Newcastle-upon-Tyne (B)
VL	Lincoln (B)
VM	Manchester (B)
VN	Yorkshire (NR)
VO	Nottinghamshire
VP	Birmingham (B)
VS	Greenock (LB)
VT	Stoke-on-Trent (B)
VU	Manchester (B)
VV	Northampton (B)
VW	Essex
VX	Essex
VY	York (B)
VZ	Tyrone
W	Sheffield (B)
WA	Sheffield (B)
WB	Sheffield (B)
WC	Essex
WD	Warwickshire
WE	Sheffield (B)
WF	Yorkshire (ER)
WG	Stirlingshire
WH	Bolton (B)
WI	Waterford (B)
WJ	Sheffield (B)
WK	Coventry (B)
WL	Oxford (B)
WM	Southport (B)
WN	Swansea (B)
WO	Monmouthshire
WP	Worcestershire
WR	Yorkshire (WR)
WS	Edinburgh (C or C)
WT	Yorkshire (WR)
WU	Yorkshire (WR)
WV	Wiltshire
WW	Yorkshire (WR)
WX	Yorkshire (WR)
WY	Yorkshire (WR)
WZ	Belfast
X	Northumberland
XA	London
XB	London

XC	London
XD	London
XE	London
XF	London

Re-allocated Marks used only with suffix letters:—

XA	Kirkcaldy (BC)
XB	Coatbridge (BC)
XC	Solihull (B)
XD	Luton (B)
XE	Luton (B)
XF	Torbay (B)
XG	Middlesbrough (B)
XH	London
XI	Belfast (B)
XJ	Manchester (B)
XK	London
XL	London
XM	London
XN	London
XO	London
XP	London
XR	London
XS	Paisley (LB)
XT	London
XU	London
XV	London
XW	London
XX	London
XY	London
XZ	Armagh
Y	Somerset
YA	Somerset
YB	Somerset
YC	Somerset
YD	Somerset
YE	London
YF	London
YG	Yorkshire (WR)
YH	London
YI	City and County of Dublin
YJ	Dundee (B)
YK	London
YL	London
YM	London
YN	London
YO	London
YP	London
YR	London
YS	Glasgow (C or C)
YT	London
YU	London
YV	London
YW	London
YX	London

YY	London
YZ	Londonderry
Z	City and County of Dublin
ZA	City and County of Dublin
ZB	Cork (County)
ZC	City and County of Dublin
ZD	City and County of Dublin
ZE	City and County of Dublin
ZF	Cork (B)
ZH	City and County of Dublin
ZI	City and County of Dublin
ZJ	City and County of Dublin
ZK	Cork (County)
ZL	City and County of Dublin
ZM	Galway
ZN	Meath
ZO	City and County of Dublin
ZP	Donegal
ZR	Wexford
ZT	Cork (County)
ZU	City and County of Dublin
ZW	Kildare
ZX	Kerry
ZY	Louth
ZZ	Dublin: for vehicles temporarily imported from abroad

INDEX

AA 37, 134, 139
Abbey Coachworks 142
Abbott, E. D. 24
Aberdeen 61
Aberystwyth 107
ACGBI 33, 100
Adlards 7
Alberford 82
Allan, C. E. 49
Allard 7
Allard, S. 7
Allerford 22
Ambulance 85
Amilcar 4
Anzac Motor Co. 86
Arbroath 11
Arbuthnot, R. K. 118
Ards 168
Argyll 120
Arnold & Comben 53
Astor, Lady 66
Athy Circuit 140
Auburn 8, 9, 81
Austin 47, 80, 88
Autocar 35, 50, 54, 56, 58
Ayrshire 35

Bagshot 18
Ballamy, L. 7
Barker 139
Barnesley 79
Barrington, Sir C. 31
Bayleys 89
Beaulieu 62
Beaulieu Road Hotel 62
Beaver 113
Bedford Buick 10, 11, 12, 13, 40
Bedfordshire 11
Belfast 49, 168
Bentley 27
Benz 2
Berkeley Square 9
Berkshire 18
Bexhill 70
Birmingham 85
Black, N. 66

Blackford, R. A. 67
Blackhawk 168
Blake, J. & Co. 35
Bognor Regis 83
Bolster, J. 133
Bonneville 92
Botallack Mine 111
Box Hill 13
Boy Scout 107
Boyce Motometer 20
Bracebridge 154
Branscombe 77
Brighton 2, 14, 56, 64, 81, 150
Briscoe 13
Broad Sanctuary 148, 151
Brocklebank, Lady 17
Brompton Road 86
Brooklands 33, 45, 54, 66, 67, 71, 134, 164
Broom, V. 20
Brown Bros. 101
Buckinghamshire 100, 173
Buehrig 9
Buick 13–28, 99, 107
Buick, D. 11
Burnley 127
Burtenshaw, George 47
Bussel 125

Cadillac 28–38, 99, 183
Camden Town 20, 179
Campbell Circuit 67
Canada 3
Cann 179
Cardiff 162
Carlton Carriage 25, 43, 131
Case 39
Cecil, Robert 102
Chalmers 40
Chalmers-Detroit 40
Charles, John 169
Chevrolet 40–43, 99, 152
Chiswick 85
Chrysler 3, 43–48, 94
Cirencester 60
Clarkson 103

Cleveland Electric 48, 49
Cliveden 66
Coachcraft 90, 143
Cobb, John 92
Cobham 142
Cole, William 115, 130
Coleman, F. 179
Colville, Sir H. 181
Continental 113
Cord 50
Cordery, J. 51, 66
Cordland, S. 147
Cork 80
Cornwall 111
Coronation Coach 3, 114
Cotesworth, Major 148
Crosby, F. Gordon 50
Crossley 3
Crown Magnetic 57, 77, 112, 130
Croydon 84
Culley, A. E. 70
Cunard 85

Dagenham 80
Daimler 2
Darracq 30, 180
Dashwood Hill 100, 160
Davis, R. P. 104
De Dietrich 104
De Dion Bouton 47
Delco 33
Delpech, R. 17
Dennis 4
de Reeder 14, 183
de Salis, H. R. 173
De Soto 47
Detroit 58
Devil's Bridge 88, 96, 98, 107
Devon 77
Dewar Trophy 33 137
Dodge 52–54, 66
Dresser, Mrs. 85
Duesenberg, A. 9
Duncan, Isadora 81
Durant 3

Durant, W. C. 11, 55, 56, 99, 158
Duryea 2, 42, 55
Duryea. J. F. 2, 56, 57

Eagle-Bott, C. 49
Ealing 66
Earls Court 119
Eason, F. 14
Eastbourne 118
Eccles 18
Edinburgh 52
Edward VIII 27
Elizabeth I, Queen 102
Elyria 84
EMF 58
England, George Ltd. 82
Entz 51
Escott 31
Essex 58–66
Essex Terraplane 66, 80, 104, 128
Euston Road 88
Evans, Lady 176
Exeter 77
Eyston, G. 168

Fairmile Inn 31
Falk, Mrs. H. V. 83
Farnham 24
Fife 53, 162, 164
Finch, C. 21
Fitzmaurice, Captain 91
Flanders 68
Flint 11
Florida 30, 99
Flower, A. I. 106
Ford 3
France 2, 7, 9, 38, 60, 68, 69, 82, 96, 158
Franklin 83, 132, 139
Freestone & Webb 134
French Horn 35
Frome 119
Frontenac 106
Fulham 17

Galley Hill 70
Galloways 161
Garford 84
Gateshead 161
General Motors 3
George V 11, 27, 42, 43, 99
George VI 27
Germany 2
Gilbert, W. S. 4, 30, 43
Gill, T. H. 17
Ginder, A. E. 100
Glasgow 120
Glidden Tours 108
Gloucester 106
GMC 85, 130

Goldin, H. 14, 86
Goodwin, F. R. 70
Gordon, Bennett 140
Graham, Paige 87
Grant 88
Great Eastern Street 147
Great West Road 91
Grim's Dyke 30
Grosvenor 114
Guildford 4

Hammersmith 115
Hammond's Patent 130, 154
Hampshire 135
Harden-Jones 35
Hardwick House 120
Harley Davidson 89
Harrington 22
Harrods 86
Harrow Weald 30
Harvey Hudson 128
Hastings 78
Hatfield House 102
Heaton Chapel 130
Herbert, Alfred 141
Hertfordshire 79
Hestercombe 30, 96, 102
Hicks, S. 172
High Wycombe 100
Hillman 80
Hoad, Mrs. 55
Holland & Holland 30
Holstein Hall 99
Honiton 147
Hooper 27
Horsham 116
Houk 130
Hounsfield, L. 64
House of Commons 103
Hove 22
Huddersfield 144
Hudson 3
Humber 60, 67, 89–91, 142, 170
Hupmobile 20, 160
Hupp, R. C. 60, 92–94, 145
Hut Hotel 160

Ilfracombe 137
Indianapolis 112
Invicta 66
Ireland 140, 142
Isle of Man 168
Iver Heath 173
Ivy Lodge 173

Jarrott & Letts 104
Jersey 40, 122
Jewett 95
Jockey Club 120, 137
Junior Car Club 67

Kalamazoo 157

Kennel Club 85
Kent, Duke of 27
Kettering, C. 37
Kew 3
King 54, 96
Knape, J. 97, 127
Knight, C. Y. 180
Knightsbridge 113
Krit 98, 123

Labourdette 139
Lake District 68
Lalique 38
Lancefield 38
Lanchester 2, 91
Langhorne, N. 66
La Salle 99
Lee, Mr. 53
Leeding, W. 172
Leland & Faulconer 28
Le Mans 168
Lendrum & Hartman 21
Lightwater 181
Lincoln 7
Little 99, 154
Liverpool 35
LNWR 71, 120, 132, 140
Locomobile 30
Locomotives on Highways Act 2, 100–104, 173
London 2, 56
London Motor Show 4, 21, 50, 71, 91, 100, 108, 113, 124, 130, 132, 139, 141, 147, 150, 179
London to Brighton 2, 166, 170
London Trotting Club 85
Lucas 9, 27
Lyme Regis 44, 77

Macfarlane Bros 125
Macklin, N. 142
Maibohm 105
Maidenhead 66
Maiflower 106
Manchester 3
Marmon 73, 106, 112, 130
Marquette 107
Martin 112
Martinsyde Motorcycle 112
Mascots 35
Maxwell 38, 66, 108
Maxwell-Briscoe 108, 109
McKenna 3
McLaughlin-Buick 27
Meadows 142
Metz 110
Michelin 28
Michigan 99
Middlesex 117, 135
Midland Hotel 85
Mill Court 183
Milnes-Daimler 49

Mitchell 110
MMC 2, 111
Monmouthshire 122
Monza 66
Mooers, L. P. 140
Moon 111
Morris 61
Mortlake Road 54, 62, 130
The Motor 39
Motor Car Club 56
Motor Show 67
Mulliner, Arthur 167
Mulliner, H. J. 113

Napier 2, 131
National 30, 112
National Motor Museum 62
New Forest 62
New York 21
Newmarket 108, 113, 154
Newport 122
Nobel Peace Prize 102
Noma 112
Norfolk Street 49
Northampton 167
Norton-sub-Hamdon 70

Oakland 86
Offord 82, 113–117, 123
Ohio 84
Olds, R. E. 105, 120
Oldsmobile 86
Olympia 50, 118–124
Opel 43, 181
Orchard Street, London 36
Osborne, William 18
Oshawa 27
Overland 3
Owen Magnetic 51, 125–129
Oxford 100

Packard 130–135
Packer, Dr. 176
Paddington 17
Paige 136
Paige-Detroit 95
Paige-Jewett 137
Pall Mall 46, 138
Panhard et Levassor 120
Paris 38, 139
Peerless 120, 139
Pennine Hills 68
Pennsylvania 156
Penrith 68
People's Refreshment 61
Perspex 62, 85
Perth 69
Peterborough 80, 89, 125
Peugeot 2
Philadelphia 171
Pierce-Arrow 140
Pitlochry 125

Plymouth 141
Polkey 182
Pontiac 117
Poole, J. L. 14
Portman, E. W. B.
Poynder, J. D. 103
Pratt 28
Prescott 7
Price, M. 106
Purcell, A. 14

RAC 33
Racine 37, 105, 130, 134
Railton 92
Railton, R. 142–144, 166
Ranalah 169
RCH 145
Reading 120
REAL 66
Red Cross 15
Regal 146
Regent Carriage 17, 147
Registrations 3
Reigate 4, 21
Reiss, F. 47, 152, 176
Reo 148–154
Reynolds Bros 79
Riley 81
Rippon 144, 160
Ritz Hotel 48
Roadmaster 28, 155, 156
Roamer 157
Rolls, R. C. 2
Rolls-Royce 35, 100
Romsey Abbey 96, 129, 139,
142, 157
Rose, C. D. 120
Rose & Crown 80
Rover 47
Royce, H. 2, 61
Royston 4, 79, 100
RSM Automobiles 9
Rugby 50, 158
Rushmore 139
Rutland Garage 140, 154

St. Helier 40
St. James's 46
St. Just in Penrith 111
St. Louis 111
Salisbury, Marquess of 102
Salmons 97
Sandusky 105
Saxon 158
Scammell 81
Scotland 120
Scottish Automobile Club 66,
125
Scottish Trials 150
Seabrook-RMC 147
Seely, J. 103
Selfridge 171

Shaftesbury Avenue 71, 72
Sharon 156
Sharpe, F. G. 150
Sharpe, H. G. 150
Shere 42
Sidcup 36
Simpson, W. 27
Singer 28
Sittingbourne 28
Somerset 31
South Woodford 106, 119, 128,
147
Southampton 78
Southgate Ltd. 105
Southport 51
Sperry 49
Spirit of Ecstasy 35
Sporting Life 85, 96
Springfield 56
Stag's Head mascot 96
Stanley 119
Stanley Cycling Club 119, 159–
161, 172
Star 70, 172
Stentophone 74, 158
Stepney 11
Stockport 3, 12, 30, 76, 90
Stormont Castle 4, 49
Strachan 154
The Strand 49
Strathpeffer 118
Studebaker 68
Sturt-Goacher 164–166
Stutz 166–169
Suffolk 154
Sunbeam 60
Surrey 32
Sussex 42, 78, 84, 99, 106, 142,
152, 164, 181
Sutton 81, 83, 117, 172, 182
Symonds, H. E. 66

Tags 3
Talbot 160
Tarrytown 108
Taunton 30
Terraplane 91
Test Hill 67, 142, 170
Texas Motor Co. 104
Thorney 80
Tourist Trophy Race 168
The Traveller's Rest 61
Triplex Safety Glass 17
Trojan 64
The Upper Crust 133

Utah 92

Vanden Plas 4
Vauxhall 3
Venables, G. L. 11, 43, 60, 183
Veteran Motorists 166

Victoria & Albert Museum 113
Vim 123, 170
Volkswagen 83, 171

Wadd, F. R. 154
Wales 107
Walker 171
Wallingford 183
Walton-on-the-Naze 104
Warland Rims 35
Warwick Wright 74, 168, 179
Waterloo Place 17, 169
Watford 81
Watney, R. 168

Waverley 49
Westminster 11
Weston 148, 151, 183
Weybridge 22
Weymann 22, 99
White 63, 131, 167, 168, 172–179
White, A. 121
White-Coleman 179
Whiting-Grant 88
Wichita 180
Wilkes-Barre 51
Willesden 135
Willys-Knight 180

Willys-Overland 128
Willys-Overland-Crossley 130
Winchester 135
Wingrove Hotel 98
Winton 181–183
Wisconsin 105
Wisley 160, 180
Wolseley 132
Wolverhampton 158
Wood's Garage 22
Woolwich 15, 99
Worth 72

Yeovil 70